GLOBAL ORGANIZATIONS

The World Trade Organization

GLOBAL ORGANIZATIONS

GLOBAL ORGANIZATIONS

The World Trade Organization

Ronald A. Reis

Series Editor
Peggy Kahn
University of Michigan–Flint

CHELSEA HOUSE
PUBLISHERS
An imprint of Infobase Publishing

The World Trade Organization

Copyright © 2009 by Infobase Publishing

All rights reserved. No part of this book may be reproduced or utilized in any form or by any means, electronic or mechanical, including photocopying, recording, or by any information storage or retrieval systems, without permission in writing from the publisher. For information contact:

Chelsea House
An imprint of Infobase Publishing
132 West 31st Street
New York NY 10001

Library of Congress Cataloging-in-Publication Data
Reis, Ronald A.
The World Trade Organization / Ronald A. Reis.
   p. cm. — (Global organizations)
Includes bibliographical references and index.
ISBN 978-0-7910-9542-3 (hardcover)
1. World Trade Organization. 2. International trade agencies. 3. International trade agencies.
I. Title. II. Series.

HF1385.R435 2008
382'.92—dc22   2008054308

Chelsea House books are available at special discounts when purchased in bulk quantities for businesses, associations, institutions, or sales promotions. Please call our Special Sales Department in New York at (212) 967-8800 or (800) 322-8755.

You can find Chelsea House on the World Wide Web at http://www.chelseahouse.com

Series design by Erik Lindstrom
Cover design by Ben Peterson

Printed in the United States of America

Bang KT 10 9 8 7 6 5 4 3 2 1

This book is printed on acid-free paper.

All links and Web addresses were checked and verified to be correct at the time of publication. Because of the dynamic nature of the Web, some addresses and links may have changed since publication and may no longer be valid.

CONTENTS

INTRODUCTION

Free Turtles—
Free Trade

THE LEATHERBACK, SO NAMED BECAUSE ITS SHELL IS LEATHERY to the touch, is a western Pacific–based sea turtle that can grow to six feet in length. Some leatherbacks weigh nearly a ton. If they are lucky (lately, luck for them has all but run out), such turtles can live 80 years or more.

Having survived the age of dinosaurs, leatherbacks may finally have reached the end of their 100-million-year run, or crawl. On the east coast of Peninsular Malaysia (normally a nesting ground for tens of thousands of hatchlings each year), the birth numbers have dwindled to an average of 10 per season. In 2006, only five nests were found, from two turtles. Not a single hatchling emerged. Today, the leatherback turtle, the largest animal of its kind, is on the verge of extinction.

Leatherbacks, at least those that remain, spend virtually their entire life at sea. Migratory patterns carry them throughout the world's oceans. Females seek land once each year to deposit their eggs on sandy beaches.

Turtle hunting, egg harvesting, and even global climate changes are key factors that have harmed the leatherback. "People sell eggs, they eat eggs, then there are the pigs and dogs that come in and dig up nests," says Kitty Simonds of the Western Pacific Regional Fishery Management Council. "Then there's development . . . hotels . . . and anything that comes close to the shore, like lights, is bad for turtles."[1]

When out to sea, which is almost always, leatherbacks often dive for jellyfish, their favorite food. These turtles have been known to descend to a depth of 3,900 feet (1,188 meters), holding their breath all the while. Although leatherbacks can stay beneath the surface for nearly half an hour while diving, they must come up to take in air. If trapped underwater, leatherbacks will drown.

They have been drowning by the thousands. Although egg hunters and scavenging pigs have taken their toll on the leatherback, it is the suffocating of turtles in the nets of trolling shrimp hunters that has brought the creatures' plight to the attention of the world and has compelled at least one country, the United States, to take the lead in combating the problem.

In 1989, in accordance with the terms of the federal Endangered Species Act of 1973, the United States Congress banned the "taking" (harassment, hunting, capturing, killing, or attempting to do any of these) of five species of sea turtles found in U.S. waters. Shrimp hunters, when fishing in areas where there was a high likelihood of encountering turtles, were required to use Turtle Excluder Devices (TEDs) to prevent the animals from becoming entangled in their nets and drowning.

A TED is essentially a grid of bars with an opening that is placed at the top or bottom of a trawl net. It acts as a trapdoor: Smaller animals, such as shrimp, pass through the bars, but larger animals, such as turtles and sharks, are ejected from the trawl when they strike the bars. According to the National Marine Fisheries Service (NMFS), "TEDs are effective at excluding up to 97% of sea turtles from shrimp nets."[2]

The U.S. law also affected countries that wished to export shrimp to the United States. If fishers of other countries did not use TEDs (where appropriate) as they gathered shrimp in their nets, their shrimp catch was banned from importation into the United States. Countries that wished to avoid this exclusion had to become certified as "turtle friendly" by the United States.

In October 1996, India, Pakistan, Thailand, and Malaysia complained. They claimed that the TED law was an unfair barrier to free trade (an open trading system with few limitations). The four Asian countries said, in effect, that the United States had no right to impose its domestic environmental values on other countries. To these countries this was a trade issue, pure and simple. The United States was seeking to exclude their products (shrimp) in a blatant protectionist effort to shield its own fishers from foreign competition.

Fortunately for the "Asian four," there was now a world body to which they could turn to for resolution: the World Trade Organization (WTO). Established in 1995 as a successor to the General Agreement on Tariffs and Trade (GATT), the WTO has the function of promoting (some would say mandating) freer trade. The WTO took up the case, and in April 1998 it ruled in favor of the Asian nations. The WTO ruling declared that the U.S. law was discriminatory and a barrier to free trade.

To environmentalists, the WTO action was no surprise. By 1998, the World Trade Organization already had become the object of resentment and animosity: It was an organization run by rich countries and beholden to multinational corporations, the environmentalists felt. Commerce was the only thing on the WTO's mind, and never mind the environment. Even though one of the richest of all countries, the United States, was, in this case, "fighting the good fight" for sea turtle survival. The WTO

On November 29, 1999, animal protection advocates wearing sea turtle costumes while carrying signs marched in protest of a WTO ruling that the U.S. Turtle-Shrimp law, which required shrimpers to use a turtle lifesaving device in their nets, as an unfair barrier to trade. A crowd of demonstrators that some say numbered over 40,000 clashed with police and the National Guard, drawing worldwide attention and giving it the name "the Battle of Seattle."

itself was, the environmentalists bemoaned, doing what it does best: forcing countries to lift barriers to the free flow of goods and services at the expense of the environment.

On further examination, however, it turns out that the initial WTO ruling against the United States was more complex and not nearly so insistent. The WTO was quick to point out just what its Appellate (review) Body said and did not say in the case. According to the WTO Web site, the international organization declared:

> We have *not* decided that the protection and preservation of the environment is of no significance to the Members of the WTO. Clearly it is.
>
> We have *not* decided that the sovereign nations that are Members of the WTO cannot adopt effective measures to protect endangered species, such as sea turtles. Clearly they can and should.
>
> And we have *not* decided that sovereign states should not act together . . . either within the WTO or in other international fora [forums], to protect endangered species or to otherwise protect the environment. Clearly they should and do.[3]

What the WTO did say, as is pointed out on its Web site, is that the measure as applied by the United States is being carried out in an arbitrary and discriminatory manner among members of the WTO.

The United States lost the case not, as some critics of the ruling supposed, because it sought to protect the environment. It lost because it discriminated among WTO members. According to the WTO, "the United States provided countries in the Western Hemisphere—mainly the Caribbean—technical and financial assistance and longer transition periods for their fishermen to start using turtle-excluder devices. It did not give the same advantage, however, to the four Asian countries

(India, Malaysia, Pakistan, and Thailand) who filed the complaint with the WTO."[4]

Under the WTO charter, a nondiscrimination clause requires that one country not impose restrictions on another country that it does not require of all other countries. The WTO determined that the United States had done just that by favoring Caribbean countries over the Asian countries.

The United States appealed the WTO decision. At the same time, it sought to conform to the WTO compliance steps designed to eliminate the discrimination. For example, the United States offered technical training in the design, construction, installation, and operation of TEDs (each of which cost from $50 to $300) to any government that requested it. As a result of such actions, the WTO reversed its earlier ruling and declared that the United States had made good-faith efforts to negotiate new, nondiscriminatory agreements.

Malaysia was not satisfied and again appealed the case, but to no avail. Malaysia never attempted to attain certification as a nation that could export shrimp to the United States. On June 15, 2001, the WTO Dispute Settlement Body upheld America's revised, although considerably weakened, turtle protection measures. Now, shrimp are allowed into the United States if they are carried there by any ship that employs turtle protection technology, regardless of whether the ship actually caught the shrimp. Critics call this "shrimp laundering."

Today, as a result of U.S. environmental polices and the efforts of many Malaysians and others who are concerned with saving sea turtles, the prospects for sea turtle survival have increased. There is no guarantee, however, that all will end well for the leatherbacks. It will be many years, perhaps 20 or 30, before efforts to revive turtle populations can be declared a success.

In this situation, the WTO comes out looking reasonably good because, ultimately, it sided with a country's right to impose environmental regulations beyond its borders. Many people around the world do not see the WTO in such a positive light, however. According to detractors, the WTO's actions in this case only illustrate that the exception (if, indeed, it can be called that) proves the rule. When taken in total, the detractors say, the international trade organization's decisions affecting the environment are almost always pro-corporate and anti-environment.

On such matters as the right of workers to a decent wage, the importation of dangerous substances, environmental degradation, the loss of national sovereignty, and antagonisms between rich countries and poor countries, activists increasingly seek to challenge the WTO in its role as champion of free trade and globalization (a closer integration of the countries of the world). Today, the WTO consists of 152 member nations, and the organization sets the rules for world trade. In 2006, that trade was valued at $17 trillion.[5] Sea turtle survival may be the least of the WTO's, and the world's, challenges in the years to come.

Traders and Raiders

WHETHER IT IS APPROACHED HEAD-ON OR IN PROFILE, THE gangly, cud-chewing camel, either single-humped (dromedary) or double-humped (Bactrian), is one goofy-looking creature. Why humans, beginning around 3000 B.C., ever chose to domesticate this hairy, plodding mammal seems, at first, to be a mystery. The camel has a single characteristic of considerable advantage, however. A camel can drink up to 50 gallons of water in a single session at a waterhole, and the precious liquid quickly courses through the animal's body as a cooling agent. Thus refreshed, a camel can march for days, or even for a week, through torrid desert terrain and not need another drop of liquid relief.

Fitted with an Arabian saddle, a camel can carry an average of 500 pounds. A "super camel," the hybridized result of a dromedary-Bactrian mix, might haul half a ton. From Morocco to India to China, these beasts, tethered together in groups of between three and six, can cover between 20 and 60 miles in one day. Having all but replaced the lowly donkey by 1500 B.C., the camel soon became the trade "vehicle" of choice throughout the Middle East and across the steppes of Asia.

For three millennia, camels carried ivory, incense, cotton, gold, and copper eastward, through Asia to far-off China. From the Spice Islands of the Moluccas in present-day Indonesia and China's Middle Kingdom came nutmeg, mace, cloves, sandalwood, porcelain, and, of course, silk.

All along the way, goods going and coming changed hands at dozens of trading posts and desert oases, and the desire to trade rather than raid asserted itself. It was, if you will, an early version of the World Trade Organization: WTO 1.0. Taxing traders and selling them safe conduct, it turned out, paid better than plundering a shrunken, fearful traffic.[6]

That said, much danger still awaited traders as they hauled their cargos across barren landscapes, over rugged hills, and through hostile populations. To reduce the hazards, men of commerce, early on, sought safer routes—ones with fewer stops and limited adverse contacts. Arabian sailing ships and oared craft plied the Mediterranean and the Red Sea, and dhows—lateen-rigged boats with hulls stitched together with coconut fiber—sailed eastward and westward through the Indian Ocean.

Not to be outdone, the Chinese soon developed a powerful and advanced merchant fleet of their own. Their vessels were constructed with nested hulls fastened with iron nails, and they contained several decks. They used effective stern-mounted rudders, boasted a magnetic compass guidance system, and featured an advanced fore-and-aft sail arrangement that enabled ships to tack almost directly into the wind.[7] Chinese naval efforts reached their zenith with the construction of the famous

A man walks past a replica of a Zheng He treasure ship at the Zheng He Treasure Boat Factory Ruins Park in Nanjing, China. Zheng sailed his well-equipped fleets to Arabia, East Africa, India, Indonesia, and Thailand (formerly Siam), trading goods along the way.

treasure fleets, which were commanded, from A.D. 1405 to 1433, by a seven-foot-tall admiral named Zheng He.

Sporting up to nine masts and dozens of spacious cabins, the largest Chinese ships were 400 feet in length and displaced up to 3,000 tons. When a flotilla of perhaps 300 vessels set sail from southern China for the Indian Ocean, bound for ports as far away as Somalia and Kenya, in East Africa, 30,000 sailors and marines were aboard.

In the seven voyages he commanded, Zheng He sought everywhere to trade, not plunder and, as he wrote, to "manifest the transforming power of virtue and to treat distant people with kindness."[8] In the late fifteenth century, however, Europeans sought to break out and capture trade routes that had been dominated by Muslims for nearly a thousand years. Soon, Admiral Zheng's "trade not raid" approach to international commerce—a course the World Trade Organization (as will be discovered) exists to promote in the modern era—was sorely tested.

SECURING WORLD TRADE ROUTES

Unexpectedly, within a few generations of Zheng's death in 1433, China pulled back from its extensive sea trading. It eventually destroyed its gargantuan ships and made the construction of new ones with two or more masts an offense punishable by death. Into the void rushed the Europeans, led by the Portuguese.

Encouraged to explore by their far-sighted monarch, Prince Henry the Navigator, Portuguese seamen sought a path to India and beyond via a route they were sure existed: around the southern tip of Africa. In 1498, Portuguese explorer Vasco da Gama rounded Africa's Cape of Good Hope and then proceeded on to Calicut (modern Kozhikode) on the west coast of the Indian subcontinent (the landmass that today holds India, Pakistan, and Bangladesh).

Because he failed to carry much in the way of trade goods, da Gama soon was sent packing back to Lisbon. In 1502, he returned to India in a sour mood. He was spoiling for a fight and eager for a takeover. According to historian Daniel Boorstin, "He [da Gama] seized a number of traders and fishermen whom he picked up casually in the harbor. He hanged them at once, then cut up their bodies, and tossed hands, feet, and heads into a boat, which he sent ashore with a message in Arabic suggesting that the Samuri use these pieces of his people to make himself a curry."[9]

Such brutality characterized the actions of the Portuguese as they advanced eastward. They sought to secure the Spice

Islands of the Moluccas and trading stations on the island of Timor and in Macau, in China. They also sought to secure a vital choke point in the Straits of Malacca, between the island of Sumatra and the Malay Peninsula. For the Portuguese, trade was to be forced at the point of a gun. This Portuguese ascendancy lasted, in places, for 100 years or more.

If sixteenth century east-west trade belonged to the Portuguese, seventeenth century trade was ruled by the Dutch. Although at times they were as cruel as their predecessors, the Dutch merchants came to the Spice Islands to trade. They also formed a company to carry on their commerce.

Known as the Dutch East India Company (in old Dutch, *Vereenigde Oost-Indische Compagnie*, or VOC), this government-granted monopoly was blessed early on with the ability to borrow money at low interest rates. In consequence, as it spread its financial risk among investors small and large, the VOC saw its capital (worth) rapidly accumulate. Thus structured, the company set out to acquire permanent bases in Asia, where it could repair and provision its ships and trade in various goods. It also sought to do business without interference from local rulers or the Portuguese.

Next, in the eighteenth century, came the British. Through their own East India Company (EIC), the British considerably expanded the exchange of goods. Grabbing a main foothold in the subcontinent, the EIC sought to import raw cotton to England and then export finished goods from its burgeoning industrial weaving centers in Manchester and throughout England. When the cotton trade played out, the EIC turned to importing tea from China. The EIC later forced that country to accept Indian opium in exchange for its tea.

At the same time, English traders traveled to the New World of the Americas and, in particular, to the Caribbean. There, colonists set up vast sugarcane plantations. To run these labor-intensive enterprises, the British turned to an entirely different kind of trade, one in human beings. Between 1519 and the end of the slave trade in the 1860s, 13 million Africans were torn from their continent in chains. At least 1.5 million of them perished in transit.

By the dawn of the nineteenth century, international trade, worldwide and still growing, encompassed both the good and the bad. There was trade in raw materials and industrial products on the one hand, and in slaves and opium on the other.

COMPARATIVE ADVANTAGE

An eighteenth-century Scotsman, Adam Smith, is perhaps the world's most famous economist. He may not have said it first, but he said it well enough, in his great work, *An Inquiry into the Nature and Causes of the Wealth of Nations* (published in 1776): "Man has an intrinsic propensity to truck, barter, and exchange one thing for another."[10] By that year, at the time of the American Revolution, people did not need to be told that trade was happening all around them. Smith was stating the obvious.

Not so for Englishman David Ricardo, however. This worthy successor to Adam Smith published his *On the Principles of Political Economy and Taxation* in 1817. In his treatise, Ricardo put forward a theory that has come to be seen as perhaps the single most important statement in all of economics. This theory also is considered the foundation on which the concept of free trade, and thus the WTO itself, is founded. It is known as the principle of comparative advantage. It took some time for the merchant class to grasp what Ricardo was saying; even today, there are those who find the concept troublesome to comprehend or accept.

The principle of comparative advantage says that a country should concentrate on producing or providing what it does best (at the lowest cost), even if it also can produce other goods and services a bit better than competing countries. Each country then should trade what it produces for what it does not have. In other words, it is better for China to concentrate on turning out DVD players, for Argentina to raise beef, for Japan to build cars, and for France to design high fashions, than for these countries to seek self-sufficiency. Countries should specialize in the areas in which they excel. In doing so, all countries will benefit, provided that they freely trade what they produce.

On a personal level, comparative advantage means that if a person is extremely good at creating Web sites, and merely good at fixing motorcycles, he should concentrate exclusively on designing fantastic Web pages even if he is better able to maintain his Harley than the mechanic down the street. Let the mechanic do the tune-up while the Web designer stays in front of his computer screen. The Web designer would experience a loss in comparative advantage in the form of the net income he would have to forgo if he were to spend time fixing his bike rather than creating Web pages.

Of course, a country may not want to put all of its eggs in a limited number of baskets. There may be strategic goods and processes that it needs to reserve for its own production and, thus, protection. Furthermore, there is always the danger of disruption to international supply chains, and competition for goods and services is never perfect. Nonetheless, the concept of comparative advantage speaks to the fundamental proposition that it is best to do what one does best, to let others do the same, and to barter and truck for what is needed.

The free-trade principle manifested itself most clearly more than 20 years after Ricardo's death. In 1845, a potato fungus attacked crops in Ireland and England, wiping out this staple foodstuff and causing widespread misery and starvation. Relief was not immediately forthcoming, in part because of Great Britain's infamous Corn Laws of the time. These laws heavily taxed imports of foreign-grown grain (the word *corn* meant, in effect, "all grains") to keep the domestic price of grains, grown by the nobility on their vast estates, high. The working class paid dearly, of course, through artificially high food prices.

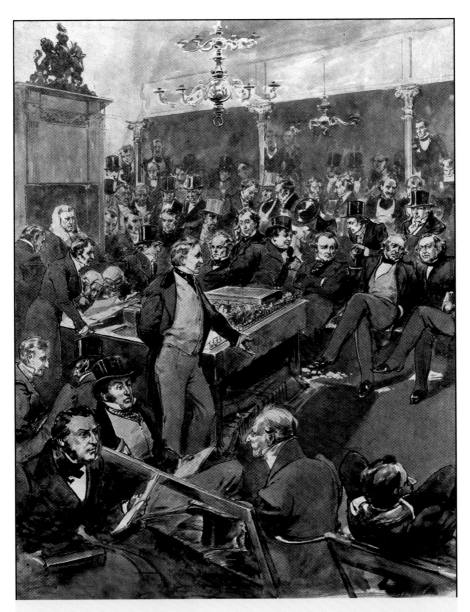

Robert Peel *(center, standing)* announces to the House of Commons in London that he supports free-trade principles during the Corn Law debate in 1846. Peel hoped that repealing the Corn Laws would free up more food for the Irish during the Irish Potato Famine (1845–1849) and spoke out, although he knew it would mean the end of his ministry.

In response to their suffering, British workers rioted for free trade. They demanded that the government repeal (withdraw) the Corn Laws and allow lower-priced grain into the country. In return, the workers agreed to pay for the imported grain with their labor, as manufacturers of bread.

In June 1846, the Corn Laws were repealed by the British Parliament. In spearheading the effort to do this, Prime Minister Robert Peel lost his job. Nevertheless, as a result, the free-trade principle took a giant leap forward. It became the dominant economic reality throughout the world until the outbreak of the First World War, nearly 70 years later.

FREE TRADE'S CHILL WIND

Using a horse-drawn contraption with cutting teeth on a rectangular frame, Nathaniel Wyeth, an enterprising New England hotelkeeper, cut chunks of ice into uniform blocks 20 inches on each side, all the better to load and stack them tightly. Working in the dead of winter, Wyeth carted the blocks from the frozen rivers and ponds of the American Northeast to ships that waited in East Coast harbors, most notably in Boston. Crammed onto the decks of sailing ships and covered with sawdust, up to 150 tons of ice could be made ready to sail on a four-month journey to far-off India. Thanks to Wyeth and his imitators, in the decade before the American Civil War, a higher tonnage of ice was shipped out of Boston harbor than any other commodity.

Americans quenched the thirst of men and women half a world away by cooling their drinks with crystal-clear New England ice, only a third of which melted in transit. This story illustrates how far the imperative to truck and barter under the principle of free trade had come by the mid-nineteenth century. The desire to exchange needed to be backed by the means to do so, of course. As the century wore on and the transition from sail to steam manifested itself on the high seas, the bartering of the world's goods multiplied enormously.

The triumph of the steamship over the sailing ship took decades to materialize and wasn't fully accomplished until the turn of the twentieth century. Competing against the newer, faster, wooden-hulled sailing ships—clippers—that were being built in New England, steamships of iron and, later, steel had a rough go of it at first.

The biggest problem facing the steamers was the need to refuel en route. A steamship either carried tons of coal to feed its boilers, thus sacrificing valuable cargo space, or had to find refueling stations along the way, thus adding time and cost to the journey. Nonetheless, with the development of more efficient engines that consumed less fuel, the advantage of steam eventually became obvious.

By the end of the nineteenth century, steam propulsion was economical on all but the longest routes. When the digging of the Suez Canal in 1869 cut the distance from London to Bombay (modern Mumbai) from 11,500 to 6,200 miles, the age of sail was all but doomed. By the time the Panama Canal opened in 1914, low-cost steam shipping was a reality everywhere. Steam powered the engine of free trade.

Free trade was to see its first major interruption, indeed a contraction, soon enough, however. From 1914 to 1918, the world (and particularly Europe) tore itself asunder in the First World War. With the advent of a worldwide Great Depression a dozen years later, the desire for protectionism (an attempt to regulate trade and subsidize domestic industries) rose in triumph. In the United States, passage of the Smoot-Hawley Tariff on June 17, 1930, exemplified this turn inward. The tariff attempted to save domestic industries from low-cost foreign competition.

Smoot-Hawley raised tariffs (fees) on more than 20,000 imported goods to record levels. The tax on 3,200 specific products and materials went to 60 percent. Other countries retaliated by slapping their own import duties (fees) on American products. Canada established new tariffs on 16 products that constituted 30 percent of all U.S. merchandise exported north of the border.[11]

The Smoot-Hawley Tariff did not cause the Great Depression; in 1929, imports represented just 4.2 percent of the United States' gross national product (the sum total of goods and services produced). The worldwide rush to protectionism and the vicious spiral downward that it instigated did put a chill on world trade, however.

A NEW INTERNATIONAL ECONOMIC ORDER

As the fourth decade of the twentieth century dragged on, depression spread around the world and the threat of a new international conflict grew. As matters became more dire, some people saw an urgent need to reverse the protectionist course and found a new world order based on the principles of freer trade. Doing so, these thinkers reasoned, not only would bring desired economic stability and greater prosperity; it also would contribute to world peace and understanding.

One man who championed this cause was an American politician, born in a log cabin in Tennessee, who went on to be the longest-serving secretary of state in American history. In 1945, he won the Nobel Peace Prize for his help in establishing the United Nations. Cordell Hull's founding belief was that trade and peace were interwoven: One contributed to and promoted the other. According to the Web site of the Cordell Hull Institute, Hull declared in 1937, "I have never faltered in my belief that enduring peace and the welfare of nations are indissolubly connected with friendliness, fairness, equality and the maximum practical degree of freedom in international trade."[12]

Hull liked to illustrate the moral value of trade by reciting stories, the most telling of which were gleaned from his childhood:

When I was a boy on the farm in Tennessee, we had two neighbors—I'll call them Jenkins and Jones—who

Cordell Hull was a distinguished member of Congress and the leader of the movement for low tariffs, as well as the author of several tax bills. In 1933, Hull was appointed secretary of state. In this role, he negotiated reciprocal trade agreements with numerous countries, lowering tariffs and stimulating trade. Pictured is Hull *(left, seated)* with U.S. president Franklin Roosevelt *(center, seated)* and Italian finance minister Guido Jung *(right, seated)* and a group of advisers.

were enemies of each other. For many years there had been bad feelings between them—I don't know why—and when they met on the road or in town or at church, they stared at each other coldly and didn't speak.

Then one of the Jenkins' mules went lame in the spring just when Jenkins needed him the most for plowing. At the same time Jones ran short of corn for hogs. Now it happened that Jones was through with his own plowing and had a mule to spare, and Jenkins had a bin filled with corn. A friendly third party brought the two men together, and Jones let Jenkins use his mule in exchange for corn for the hogs.

As a result, it wasn't long before the two old enemies were the best of friends. A common-sense trade and ordinary neighborliness had made them aware of their economic need for each other and brought them peace.[13]

Jenkins and Jones, in other words, discovered that they were worth more to each other alive than dead.

In 1944, as the Second World War pressed toward its conclusion, representatives of the United States and Great Britain met in the sleepy New England town of Bretton Woods to hammer out an agreement to reverse the protectionism of the previous decades, to expand international trade, and to establish binding rules on economic activity in general.

To carry out their ambitious plan, the delegates at Bretton Woods agreed to form three international organizations. In 1945, the International Monetary Fund (IMF) was created to administer the international monetary (money) system. Beginning in 1946, the International Bank for Reconstruction and Development, later known as the World Bank, provided loans for Europe's reconstruction and, eventually, assisted developing countries. In 1947, the General Agreement on Tariffs and Trade (GATT) was established as a global trade organization; it was charged with fashioning and enforcing multilateral (that is, multi-nation) trade agreements. Almost a half-century later (1995), the World Trade Organization, with greatly expanded powers, emerged from the GATT.

Globalization

HE IS THE SECOND MOST RECOGNIZED CHARACTER IN AMERICA,
exceeded in popularity only by Santa Claus. Worldwide,
the corporate symbol that Ronald McDonald represents, the
Golden Arches, is more readily identified than the Christian
cross. At the turn of the twenty-first century, the fast-food giant
had franchised no less than 30,000 restaurants, in places that
range from the highways of the United States to the cities of
sub-Saharan Africa. As a symbol of American corporate expansion and cultural and economic penetration, the globalization
of McDonald's has few equals.[14]

McDonald's founder, Ray Kroc, once said of his rivals, "If
they were drowning I'd put a hose in their mouth."[15] Today, the
enterprise is ranked 217 on *Forbes*'s "Global 2000," with sales

McDonald's, which was founded in 1940, now has more than 31,000 restaurants worldwide. In an effort to satisfy public demands for ethical products, McDonald's began sourcing all their coffee beans from farms certified by the Rainforest Alliance, a nonprofit group working to give farmers in developing countries sustainable livelihoods. *Above*, a McDonald's in Tokyo's Shibuya shopping district.

of $22,787,000,000 in 2007.[16] McDonald's, as American as the hamburger itself, is everywhere.

And then there's Pollo Campero (Spanish for "country chicken"). Not yet the size of McDonald's, even in its domestic market of Guatemala, this Central American restaurant chain has, nonetheless, gone international. It entered the United States in 2002. After selling 3 million takeout orders in its Central American airport stores, mainly to hungry travelers bound for the United States to visit relatives, the company decided to go global. "Our roots are Latin American, but our restaurant is for everybody," said Pollo Campero spokesman Robert Lasala to United Press International. "All nationalities are welcome."[17]

Food is not the only Latin American export making its way onto the world stage. "Salsa has become the biggest international dance craze since the advent of rock 'n' roll in the 1950s, and dwarfs even the popularity of tango during the 1920s," reports the London-based newspaper *The Economist*. "Almost every city in Europe now has a cluster of clubs offering classes at all levels, with Britain, Germany, and Scandinavia especially well-served."[18] If globalization is, in part, about shifting forms of human contact, salsa, with its fast, intimate embrace between partners, is out there leading the charge.

Certainly, globalization, a closer integration of the countries of the world, takes many forms, ranging from the social and cultural to the political and economic. Remittances—sums of money sent home to families in undeveloped countries by migrants who work in developed nations—involve, for example, all four of these aspects of globalization. In 2007, nearly $240 billion moved from rich lands to poor lands.[19]

Although a construction worker from Bangladesh who works in Dubai, United Arab Emirates, on the tallest tower in the world may earn just $1 per hour, that wage is a lot better than the $1 a day his compatriot back home makes as he tends a rice paddy. By sending home half his salary, the laborer in Dubai who swings crossbeams into place a thousand feet above the desert sand can make all the difference to a family barely subsisting in Bangladesh. When Ann Sanchez, slinging fish tacos at a stall in the Grand Central Market in downtown Los Angeles, sent $1,500 home to Mexico in 2007, that individual source of foreign exchange was roughly equivalent to an average annual salary in that country, with its minimum wage of about $4.65 per day.[20]

Coming and going—here, there, and everywhere—goods, services, and labor are all part of today's globalization, the phenomenon of our time.

AN INTERCONNECTED WORLD

Globalization, whether through finance, travel, communications, cultural penetration, or trade, is, in effect, all about connectivity: the closer integration of the countries and peoples of the world. Although the phenomenon of globalization has been with us, to varying degrees, for thousands of years, it is in the post–World War II period, and particularly since 1980, that globalization has become all-pervasive and encompassing. With the enormous reductions in the cost of communication and transportation that have taken place in the past 25 years, the barriers to the flow of capital, goods, services, knowledge, and people also have fallen. In turn, new international organizations, such as the World Trade Organization, have emerged to facilitate the integration of our world.

Many formal definitions of globalization exist. This one, from economist Manfred B. Steger, is particularly relevant:

> Globalization refers to a multidimensional set of social processes that create, multiply, stretch, and intensify worldwide social interdependencies and exchanges while at the same time fostering in people a growing awareness of deepening connections between the local and the distant.[21]

That such interconnectivity exists, there can be no doubt. The global labor force has risen fourfold since the beginning of the 1980s. Globalization of labor has led to a strong expansion in trade, with such trade growing by an average of 7.1 percent annually since 1980. World trade has almost sextupled in less than a generation.

Foreign direct investment has exploded, too. In 1980, it stood at US$55 billion. By 2005, it had climbed to almost one trillion dollars (US$916 billion). Money, goods, and people are ranging the globe.[22]

Of course, there are pros and cons to what is happening—to the increase in social integration and economic activity worldwide. On the plus side:

- Individuals have more access to products of different countries.
- Developing countries have seen increased cash flows as an aid to development.
- There is a greater exchange of information between countries.
- Cultural intermingling has increased.
- Socially, the peoples of the world have become more tolerant and open to one another.

On the minus side:

- The outsourcing of jobs from developed economies to emerging economies has hurt many people in the industrial West.
- Multinational corporations have grown in size and power; increasingly, they call the shots in the distribution of goods and services.
- Social degeneration and the spread of communicable diseases are clearly downsides to increased globalization.

For all the controversy surrounding globalization, however, its reality has earned a remarkably high degree of support from ordinary citizens around the world. The Pew Global Attitudes Project surveyed 38,000 people in 44 countries and concluded, "Generally, peoples of the world agree—albeit to different degrees—that after experiencing globalization through trade,

OUTSOURCING ON THE FLY

Traveling across town for routine auto maintenance may not seem much of a stretch for someone who wants expert car care at a reduced price. But flying a commercial aircraft out of the country for the same type of service certainly is going a step, or quite a few miles, further. Increasingly, however, that is what U.S. airline companies are doing as they seek to lower their maintenance costs in the face of rising fuel prices. Flying a jet to El Salvador, to Aeroman—a 1,300-employee, fully approved Federal Aviation Administration (FAA) facility—for servicing can save a U.S. carrier as much as 30 percent on maintenance bills. Such upkeep, known as Maintenance, Repair, and Overhaul (MRO), is already a huge business—one that is expected to reach nearly $60 billion worldwide within a decade.

According to Marla Dickerson, a *Los Angeles Times* staff writer, all Aeroman mechanics speak at least some English, the language in which all paperwork for the FAA must be completed. An experienced Salvadoran mechanic can make $1,000 per month, plus $120 monthly in bonuses. In a country in which the minimum wage for service workers is about $175 per month, that is an impressive income.

Considered a first-class facility by any standards, the Aeroman operation is at El Salvador International Airport, about 30 miles finance, travel, communications, and culture, they favor an interconnected world."

Even when confronted with economic and social problems in their lives, people are less likely to blame globalization than to recognize the positives. This is particularly true with regard to the economic aspects of globalization. The Pew survey found

south of San Salvador, the capital city. The facility welcomes frequent, unannounced FAA inspectors. "We are used to being constantly under surveillance," Andres Garcia, the commercial director for Aeroman, told the *Los Angeles Times*. Aeroman's 600 mechanics are rigorously trained and hold Salvadoran licenses recognized by the European Aviation Safety Agency. About 100 of the mechanics hold FAA certificates.

Luis Barrera is one such mechanic. "It's interesting work," he told Dickerson. "And it's a big responsibility. . . . We always try to do things in the best way. Our families fly too."

Unionized mechanics in the United States resent such outsourcing, whereby jobs traditionally done by Americans now are done overseas. These mechanics claim that the United States is not only losing good jobs but also potentially putting passengers at risk. Such outsourcing is here to stay, however. As an American worker loses a job, a Salvadorian worker (in this case) gains one. Globalization has both winners and losers.

Marla Dickerson, "U.S. Airlines Flock to Foreign Repair Shops," *Los Angeles Times*, April 30, 2008. C1, C5.

that in 41 of the 44 nations studied, majorities think growing trade and business ties are good both for their country and for their families.[23]

MARKET FUNDAMENTALISM AND ITS DISCONTENTS

A famous African proverb speaks poignantly to the way the world is said to work, at least according to those who champion unregulated globalization and its competitive rules. The proverb goes something like this:

> Every morning in Africa, a gazelle wakes up.
> It knows it must run faster than the fastest lion or it will be killed.
> Every morning a lion wakes up.
> It knows it must outrun the slowest gazelle or it will starve to death.
> It doesn't matter whether you are a lion or a gazelle.
> When the sun comes up, you better start running.[24]

The dog-eat-dog, or, in this case, lion-eat-gazelle philosophy expressed in the proverb—a philosophy which says that competition is ruthless and there will be clear winners and losers—pretty much summarizes the way champions of the new global order, an order that advocated free trade, saw things in the 1980s. U.S. president Ronald Reagan and U.K. prime minister Margaret Thatcher spoke out loudly and forcefully for a free-market ideology, one based on what came to be known as market fundamentalism. The two world leaders advocated economic liberalization: the removal of government interference in financial markets and capital markets, and the removal of barriers to free trade.

To Reagan, Thatcher, and their supporters, deregulation was to be carried out on a worldwide scale, come what may. Even as such supercapitalists claimed that the results would benefit all—that "a rising tide would lift all boats," as the saying goes—it was clear to others that many millions of people would suffer in the free-market version of globalization, in a world in which there was little in the way of a safety net to soften the impact of unrestrained competition.

Although some conservatives think that what supposedly is good enough for the United States should be good enough for the world, a closer look at American history shows no such unfettered economic philosophy in our past. Indeed, as the United States expanded in the nineteenth and early twentieth centuries, as transportation and communication costs fell, the national government took an active role in shaping and regulating the new economy. According to Nobel Prize–winning economist Joseph Stiglitz, "The federal government began to regulate the financial system, set minimum wages and working conditions, and eventually provided unemployment and welfare systems to deal with the problems posed by a market system."[25]

During the Great Depression of the 1930s, there were those in the United States who insisted that by letting the free market work, its self-regulating mechanisms (Adam Smith's so-called "invisible hand") would, in time, return economic prosperity to the nation. President Franklin Roosevelt, however, heeded the call of liberal British economist John Maynard Keynes and so thought otherwise. To both men, government intervention was required.

Today, there are many who insist that, just as Keynes saved capitalism in the 1930s by advocating a degree of regulation and control, the world now needs a similar reform to see globalization benefit a wider populus. Like capitalism, they declare, globalization must be managed.

INDIA'S KILLING FIELDS

The headline in *The Economist* required a double take, or at least a second look: "Is Globalisation Killing India's Cotton

Farmers?" At first glance, a reader of the headline might think that the word *killing* refers, figuratively, to driving farmers off their land, forcing them to give up and, perhaps, head to crowded cities to find work. In reality, however, the word is to be taken literally. From mid-2005 to the end of 2006, no fewer than 1,200 farmers in Vidarbha, the cotton bowl of India, took their own lives to escape debts owed to moneylenders.

Most Westerners are well aware of India's success in attracting high-tech jobs to urban centers such as Bangalore, where tens of thousands of smart, well-trained Indians staff call centers and develop sophisticated software programs. The median income for the country as a whole, however, is just $2.70 a day.

Yet the farmers of Vidarbha, along with the tech workers of Bangalore, have, like it or not, become part of the world economy. The farmers are forced to borrow money at punitive rates to pay for the equipment necessary to sink wells and to buy costly biotech-derived cottonseeds. When fuel prices for diesel pumps soar and the new seeds prove ill-suited to the farmers' plots of land, the crops fail. "A man loses hope," says M.S. Swaminathan, the father of India's green revolution. "He has the moneylender waiting at the door every day and taunting him."[26]

As the *Economist* article points out, none of this is necessarily globalization's fault. Nonetheless, with American cotton highly subsidized and India's textile industry only too happy to purchase cheap fibers, the farmers are squeezed. With few jobs available in the cities and no social safety net for those working the land, farmers are left clinging to their marginal patches of land, or worse.

Of the 6.6 billion people who occupy planet Earth, it is estimated that 2.8 billion live on less than $2 per day. These people are known as the middling poor. Approximately half of that number, 1.2 billion, live on about $1 per day (taking inflation into account, actually about $1.25 per day), the common measure of absolute poverty. The truly desperate, those who live on less than 50 cents a day, are in danger of succumbing—that is, dying—at any time.

In Zambia, an extremely poor southern African country in which the dollar-per-day figure holds true, this means that a poor person cannot afford to buy, as a daily food ration, at least two or three plates of *nshima* (porridge), a few spoonfuls of oil, a sweet potato, a handful of ground nuts, and a couple of teaspoons of sugar, plus a banana and a chicken twice a week.

Pro-globalists rightly point out that, as bad as these numbers are, the situation worldwide actually is getting better. They claim that this improvement is, in no small part, a result of globalization.

According to World Bank figures, between 1981 and 2001, the number of people who lived on $1 per day or less fell from 1.5 billion to 1.1 billion in absolute terms.[27] Globalization backers assert that the greatest declines occurred in economies that rapidly reduced barriers to trade and investment. The percentage of those who live on less than $2 per day also has decreased, supporters point out: Globalist countries such as China have seen a 50-percent decrease in people living at this level, even as sub-Saharan Africa, a region less globally connected, has seen a 2.2 percent increase.[28]

It is doubtful that many Vidarbha cotton farmers have heard of globalization, much less the World Trade Organization. Yet what WTO members decide with regard to subsidies and trade can, as will be seen, have a profound effect on the lives (and possible deaths) of such farmers.

WINNERS AND LOSERS

Helen Buyaki is a Kenyan rose picker—a very careful one. One of 1,800 employees at the 60-acre Longonot horticulture farm in Kenya's Rift Valley, Buyaki takes roses from a cold room, cuts them to a standard length of 20.5 inches, removes leaves and thorns, bunches them, and wraps them, complete with a tiny plant-food package. Within two days, 63,000 rose stems

Kenya, the largest producer of roses in the world, is dependent on the flower industry for foreign exchange, but ethnic violence has virtually paralyzed the East African country. The Kenya Flower Council estimates that the industry lost more than $100 million in 2008. There has been an international push to buy Kenyan roses in order to support the flower growers who continue to work hard under political crisis.

will be in Europe: 70 percent of what Longonot exports each morning. By the fifth day, the roses will be in supermarkets. With a four-day shelf life and a seven-day guarantee given to buyers, the Kenyan roses must remain salable for just over two weeks, anywhere in the world.[29]

Kenya growing roses for export to far-off lands! Why not? The climate is right, the land is good, and workers like Buyaki are glad for the jobs they have. Although Buyaki earns just US$70 per month—the equivalent of seven bunches of roses that sell for $10 each at destination supermarkets—she does not feel exploited. Because of globalization, Buyaki and her fellow workers have jobs they otherwise never would have had.

Furthermore, because Longonot Horticulture has worked to acquire fair-trade certification from the International Fair Trade Association, an organization that insists that workers be treated fairly, those who purchase Longonot roses understand that what they are getting, according to Roger Cohen from the *New York Times*, is a "socially and ethically acceptable rose." Buyaki, in turn, receives free health care, among other benefits.

Although globalization has given poor countries such as Kenya access to world markets, thereby giving such countries something to trade for much-needed cash or imports, concerns about the effects of globalization remain. Even as there are winners in the global market for goods and services, there are also losers, and something must be done to confront this situation. According to economist Joseph Stiglitz, at least five anxieties can readily be identified:

One, the rules of the game are unfair. They clearly benefit advanced industrial countries over developing ones.

Two, globalization tends to advance material values over other values, such as concern for the environment.

Three, with the way globalization has been managed, developing countries find themselves with obligations to wealthier, more advanced nations.

Four, although advocates of globalization claim that, eventually, all people will benefit from freer trade and a more interconnected world, there are many losers, in both rich and poor countries.

Five, globalization often can mean Americanization, both economic and cultural. In developing countries, this rarely is seen as a good thing.[30]

As the facilitator of globalization, the WTO has been, and is, required to confront these and a host of other issues. Before we turn to such concerns as the environment, worker rights, public safety, intellectual property rights, and the rich country–poor country divide, however, we first must explore the origins of the WTO, its basic operating principles, its dispute-settlement processes, and the way its decisions are reached. We must, in short, examine the inner workings of the WTO.

The World Trade Organization Takes the Stage

REPRESENTATIVES OF THE VICTORIOUS ALLIES KNEW THAT IT would not be easy to bring world economic order out of the chaos and destruction of World War II. In the conflict's aftermath, the United States and its war-devastated European partners sensed an opportunity, however. A concerted attempt to stabilize the world's monetary supplies, to rebuild Europe, and to liberalize international trade required the establishment of new economic institutions. In July 1944, even before the war ended, delegates from the United States and Great Britain met in Bretton Woods, New Hampshire, to begin hammering out agreements to create three pillars of a workable economic system.

The International Monetary Fund (IMF) was to administer the world's monetary system. This was the organization charged with preventing another global depression. Nations

During the Bretton Woods Conference *(above)*, agreements were signed to create the International Monetary Fund, the International Bank for Reconstruction and Development, and the General Agreement on Tariffs and Trade. The purpose of the conference was to encourage open markets and to lower barriers to international trade and the movement of capital.

that were found to be letting their economies slump were to be pressured by the IMF to increase economic growth. If such countries could not stimulate aggregate demand on their own, they were to be offered loans to get their economies going.

Today, the IMF consists of 185 member countries and has its headquarters in Washington, D.C. The IMF director is always a European, a condition agreed on when the organization was established. In exchange for this requirement, the voting rules are structured in such a way that the United States, with its enormous economic clout, has sole veto power to nix any IMF measure put forward that it does not like.

There has been much criticism about the way the IMF has conducted itself since its founding over 60 years ago. The IMF was charged with the job of reducing global financial instability, but critics claim that the fund's free-market, probanking polices often have contributed to the very thing the organization was supposed to prevent. Countries now are eager to pay off their loans as soon as possible to avoid being in the grip of the IMF forever.

The World Bank also was created at Bretton Woods. It was known originally as the International Bank for Reconstruction and Development. Significantly, the word *Development* was added at the last moment, almost as an afterthought. In the immediate postwar years, the bank's focus remained almost exclusively on providing aid to war-torn Europe.

When the United States' Marshall Plan pumped billions of dollars into Europe during the late 1940s and early 1950s, the World Bank shifted its focus to that of building the infrastructure of Europe's former colonies. Today, the bank concentrates on providing loans to underdeveloped and developing countries across the globe, regardless of any former colonial status. Like the IMF, the World Bank consists of 185 members and has its headquarters in Washington, D.C. Its president is always an American. That decision was made in 1944, at the same time as the agreement that gave European leadership to the IMF.

With two pillars of a new economic order now in place, all that remained was to create a viable multilateral trade regime. To do this proved to be much harder than to agree on monetary and redevelopment matters. Indeed, it took another 50 years before a true multilateral entity, the WTO, materialized to govern international trade.

THE GATT SUBSTITUTE

The name was simple enough: the International Trade Organization (ITO). When it was proposed, along with the IMF and the World Bank, the ITO represented an attempt to establish the world's third economic pillar. Certainly, an institution was needed to regulate trade and set ground rules. Yet the ITO never came to be. As American diplomat Richard Gardner declared, "It did not have a chance to die; it was simply stillborn."[31]

Despite America's leading role in pushing to create the ITO, by 1948 it was clear that conservatives in Congress would never ratify an agreement establishing the organization. They, along with their corporate allies, were fearful that the ITO— burdened, in their eyes, with excessive regulation—would infringe on national sovereignty. To these critics, the ITO would be too intrusive; it would dictate domestic policy on many fronts, such as fair labor practices. Without U.S. support, the ITO did not stand a chance. In 1950, President Harry S. Truman announced that he would not submit the ITO Charter to Congress for ratification.

Because the Truman administration knew full well that ITO ratification was problematic, it proposed, at the same time, that a multilateral commercial treaty on tariff reductions be negotiated. The negotiation of this treaty would be led by the advanced industrial nations. Such a treaty, the administration felt, would not require congressional approval. The treaty, known as the General Agreement on Tariffs and Trade (GATT), was established in 1948. Signed by 23 countries, the agreement was meant to be temporary; it would last only until the ITO might come into effect. As it turned out, the GATT lasted for 47 years.

From 1948 to 1995, the GATT system operated on a key principle that was carried over with the formation of the WTO in 1995. Known as the nondiscrimination, or most favored nation, principle, it is, at first glance, contradictory. Although the term *most favored nation* suggests that some nations get special treatment, in reality, the exact opposite is the case. The most favored nation principle means that each country will treat all other countries the same; all will be the most favored.

This nondiscrimination principle also incorporates what is known as national treatment. According to this concept, foreign producers are to be treated the same as domestic producers. In other words, imported goods, once they enter a country, cannot be discriminated against just because they are foreign.

The GATT operated through the establishment of a series of trade rounds (negotiations). Sometimes lasting for years, such rounds sought to hammer out agreements among participants to lower tariffs and open markets, and to do so on a reciprocal basis. Throughout its existence, the GATT focused on the liberalization of trade in manufactured goods, to the comparative advantage of advanced industrial countries. Liberalization of trade was much more limited in products, such as textiles and agricultural commodities—something that would have helped developing nations.

The GATT's last round of trade negotiations began in Uruguay in 1986 and ended in Morocco in 1994. Under the final agreement, the GATT, which at the time had grown to 128 members, was to be replaced with the WTO.

The WTO was to be based in Geneva, as had been the GATT. The WTO was to occupy the same facilities as the GATT, and the GATT's director-general was to become the WTO's first director-general. Although the WTO seemed to be an extension of the GATT, it soon became apparent that the WTO was to be a great deal more than the GATT ever was or could have hoped to be.

PRINCIPLES AND ORGANIZATION OF THE WTO

In addition to the fundamental principle of nondiscrimination that the WTO inherited from the GATT, four additional principles form the foundation on which the WTO now operates.

The principle of reciprocity—also a GATT-derived principle—requires countries to make concessions: They have to agree to lower tariffs and nontariff barriers (such as import

(continues on page 48)

PASCAL LAMY: LEADING THE WTO

Every four years, a director-general is appointed by the Ministerial Conference to oversee the negotiation and implementation of new trade agreements and to police member countries' adherence of those agreements. In 2005, France's Pascal Lamy was chosen as the fifth director-general of the WTO.

A graduate of the prestigious Sciences Po school in Paris, Lamy started his career in civil service and quickly became the adviser to Jacques Delors, then president of the European Commission. Lamy became known as "the Exocet," named after the missile built in his homeland. Lamy ran Delors' office "with a rod of iron" and was known to banish those who crossed him to less pleasant European posts. Lamy served with Delors during his entire time at the commission, then briefly worked in business at Crédit Lyonnais, where he rose to the level of second in command.

His appointment as European Trade Commissioner in 2000 came as a bit of a surprise, considering his reputation for being blunt, and some thought that Lamy might alienate Europe's trading partners with his no-nonsense approach.

WTO Director-General Pascal Lamy

Instead, he was an adept negotiator, being the first top-level trade official to propose a plan to restart the talks that collapsed during the WTO Ministerial Conference of 1999 in Seattle, Washington. With his encouragement, negotiations commenced in Doha, Qatar, in 2001. This round was set to conclude in four years, in December 2005, in anticipation of two more ministerial conferences producing a final draft agreement on the Doha Round objectives. Unfortunately, these talks also failed. In fact, eight years after the Doha Round, negotiations are still ongoing.

Before the most recent conference at the WTO's headquarters in Geneva, Switzerland, on July 21, 2008, Pascal Lamy—who had been appointed the organization's director-general in 2005—said that the odds of success were over 50 percent. Although after one week of negotiations many considered an agreement within reach, once again negotiations collapsed over issues of agricultural trade among the United States, India, and China. The countries disagreed over the threshold of the special safeguard mechanism (SSM)—which allows countries to protect poor farmers by imposing a tariff on imports of specific goods if the price of those goods drops or there is a surge in imports. The United States argued that the threshold had been set too low. Lamy said, "Out of a to-do list of 20 topics, 18 had seen positions converge but the gaps could not narrow on the 19th—the special safeguard mechanism."[*] Several countries blamed each other for the breakdown and the EU trade commissioner, Peter Mandelson, characterized the collapse as a "collective failure."[**]

Besides the failure of the Doha rounds, Lamy faces deep-seated differences between Europe and the United States over the American view (one backed by other exporting countries) that farm goods should be treated like any other trade item. Officials

(continues)

(continued)

have called his subtle management between dissenting factions a "highly pleasant surprise." On December 17, 2008, Lamy told the Trade Negotiations Committee that concluding the round would be the main focus of the WTO in 2009, as well as monitoring trade measures taken in relation to the financial crisis.***

---

* "Remember Doha?: An Opportunity to Cheer Up the World Economy," *The Economist*, July 17, 2008. Available online at *http://www.economist.com/opinion/displaystory.cfm?story_id=11750413*.

** "Dismay at Collapse of Trade Talks," *BBC News*, July 30, 2008. Available online at *http://news.bbc.co.uk/2/hi/business/7532302.stm*.

*** "WTO to Move Quickly on Wider Front in 2009—Lamy," *WTO News*, December 18, 2008. Available online at *http://www.wto.int/english/news_e/news08_e/tnc_dg_stat_17dec08_e.htm*.

(continued from page 45)

bans and quotas) to obtain the same concessions for their exports to other countries. When a country knows that such concessions must be made, it can be assumed that the necessity of making them will render the country somewhat more palatable to protectionist interests at home. In other words, a government can say, when it denies protection to special interests, "The WTO made us do it."

When countries join the WTO, they agree to "bind" their commitments—that is, not to increase a rate of duty beyond an agreed level. Once a rate of duty is bound, it may not be raised without compensating the affected party. In other words, binding establishes a "ceiling." A country can change its binding, but only after negotiating with its trading partners. As a result, the partners may demand compensation for a loss of trade. Binding is clearly another important WTO principle.

Transparency is a WTO principle that has raised much controversy. Although the organization, as required, publishes its trade regulations, it often does so after the fact. The WTO's actual trade negotiations generally are closed to all but a select few.

Finally, there is a safety valve principle. Paradoxically, this principle allows governments, under certain circumstances, to restrict trade. Governments may do so under this principle when seeking to attain non-economic objectives, to ensure fair competition, and to intervene in trade for economic reasons.

The WTO is governed through ministerial conferences. These meet every two years in various parts of the world. Until 2007, there had been seven such conferences. Some, like the third one, which was held in Seattle, Washington, in 1999, have been contentious and have drawn protesters from near and far. The Ministerial Conference is the topmost decision-making body of the member-driven WTO. Those who participate in conference deliberations are led by the trade ministers of member countries.

In addition to conferences, there also are trade rounds, in which tough and tedious negotiations are supposed to lead to ever-freer trade. Since the creation of the GATT in 1947–1948, there have been eight such rounds. As has been noted, some have dragged on for years. Technically, the so-called Doha "development" Round is still in progress, though negotiations broke off in the middle of 2008. The Doha Round began back in November of 2001, at a ministerial conference held in Doha, Qatar. This round is supposed to cover issues of particular interest to developing countries, such as agriculture, labor standards, the environment, transparency, and patents. Although most observers agree that the Doha Round has been more open than previous WTO trade rounds, what its final outcome will be remains to be seen.

WTO Organizational Chart

Ministerial Conference

General Council meeting as
Trade Policy Review Body

General Council

General Council meeting as
Dispute Settlement Body

**Appellate Body
Dispute Settlement Panels**

**Doha Development Agenda:
TNC and its Bodies**

Trade Negotiations Committee

Special Sessions of
Service Council
TRIPS Council
Dispute Settlement Body
Agriculture Committee
Cotton Sub-Committee
Trade and Development Committee
Trade and Environment Committee

Negotiating groups on
Market Access
Rules
Trade Facilitation

Council for Trade in Services

Committees on
Trade in Financial Services
Specific Commitments

Working parties on
State-Trading Enterprises

Plurilaterals
Trade in Civil Aircraft Committee
Government Procurement Committee

Council for Trade-Related Aspects of Intellectual Property Rights

Council for Trade in Goods

Committees on
Market Access
Agriculture
Sanitary and Phytosanitary Measures
Technical Barriers to Trade
Subsidies and Countervailing Measures
Anti-Dumping Practices
Customs Valuation
Rules of Origin
Import Licensing
Trade-Related Investment Measures
Safeguards

Working parties on
State-Trading Enterprises

Plurilaterals
Information Technology Agreement Committee

Committees on
Trade and Environment
Trade and Development
Subcommittee on Least-Developed Countries
Regional Trade Agreements
Balance of Payments Restrictions
Budget,Finance and Administration

Working parties on
Accession

Working groups on
Trade, debt and finance
Trade and technology transfer
(Inactive:
Relationship between Trade and Investment
Interaction between Trade and competition Policy
Transparency in Government Procurement)

Key

━━━ Reporting to General Council (or a subsidiary)

━━━ Reporting to Dispute Settlement Body

▪▪▪▪ Plurilateral committees inform the General Council of Goods Council of their activities, although these agreements are not signed by all WTO members

●●●● Trade Negotiations Committee reports to General Council

(All WTO members may participate in all councils, committees, etc., except Appellate Body, Dispute Settlement panels, and plurilateral committees.
The General Council also meets as the Trade Policy Review Body and Dispute Settlement Body.

The WTO, which today consists of 153 nations, seeks—through its core principles, its administrative ministerial conferences, and, most importantly, its rounds of trade negotiations—to set the rules for world trade. The organization is ever mindful to expand such trade whenever and wherever it can.

To accomplish its mission, the WTO was, almost from its start, given powers far beyond those of its predecessor, the GATT. Today, in the eyes of many people, the WTO is the GATT on steroids.

THE ALL-POWERFUL WTO

Although there has been continuity in the move from the GATT to the WTO, the World Trade Organization differs markedly from its precursor in at least five ways. In every case, the WTO has substantially greater authority to govern international trade, to set enforcing rules, and to punish offenders.

First, the WTO provides the legal and institutional framework for the conduct of trade relations among its members. Its rules are binding. If, at the end of any integrated dispute settlement process, there is no other way to resolve issues, multilaterally authorized trade sanctions can be imposed. Paradoxically, perhaps, for a trade organization, the WTO punishes a wayward nation by restricting trade.

Second, unlike the GATT, which was provisional, the WTO is an organization in its own right, and it requires member countries to accept its rules—all of them. Countries no longer can appeal to preexisting domestic legislation to avoid adhering to WTO agreements. Even if to do so involves amending its own

(Opposite page) The WTO has 153 members (95 percent of total world trade) and is headquartered in Geneva, Switzerland. The WTO is governed by a ministerial conference, a general council, and the director-general. Its members are currently working to settle new trade negotiations called the Doha Development Agenda.

domestic laws, a member nation must do whatever it takes to comply with WTO rulings or risk retaliation. Many countries see this WTO requirement as an attack on their sovereignty.

Third, all WTO agreements are held together by a "single understanding." This means that participating countries cannot selectively apply the range of agreements within the WTO. They cannot cherry-pick—decide what they like or do not like and choose accordingly. With the WTO, each deal is an all-or-nothing deal.

Fourth, the WTO goes well beyond national borders. It penetrates deep within a country to affect a multitude of trade- and commerce-related issues. With regard to trade, the GATT was a traditional entity that dealt with trade in goods. The WTO does much more. In addition to goods, it covers such factors as services, trade-related intellectual property rights (TRIPs), and trade-related investment measures (TRIMs). Critics see this as yet another threat to national sovereignty.

Finally, the WTO has a significantly stronger dispute settlement mechanism (DSM) than the GATT ever had. The WTO enjoys what is known as the rule of negative consensus. This means that if a WTO panel's findings are to be overruled, there must be a consensus to overrule. Under the GATT, it was the other way around: There had to be a consensus to adopt a panel ruling. Thus, under the GATT, a losing party could block a ruling.

The WTO has rules that are more intrusive, more formalized, and clearly more enforceable than those of the GATT. As international trade expert Amrita Narlikar points out, "The organizational structure of the WTO . . . builds on some old GATT features but formalizes and legalizes them in a way so unprecedented that the resulting change is a qualitative one."[32]

THE WTO AND REALPOLITIK

Given all the rules, restrictions, and outright demands made by the WTO, it is fair to ask, "Why are countries desperate to join the organization; why do they stand in line to seek accession [admission]?" After all, it is not that easy to get in; in fact, it is anything but easy.

To join, a country first must complete a lengthy application. In the application, the country describes in detail all aspects of its trade and economic policies that may be of relevance to the WTO.

Second, the applicant has to tell interested parties (other countries) what it is willing to give up, in terms of trade concessions, to enter the WTO.

Third, the list of the member-to-be's commitments are drawn up by the WTO.

Finally, two-thirds of the WTO's member states must vote in favor of acceptance for admission to be offered to the applicant.

The process may not end there. In many cases, a country's own legislature or parliament has to ratify the agreement before WTO membership is complete.

This accession process can take years. Some of the world's major economic and political players, such as Russia, still are queuing up to get in. Why go through all the hassle? As Amrita Narlikar points out:

> Members assume that the cost of accession, as well as some questionable decision-making procedures and politicized negotiation processes, will be easily outweighed by the benefits of belonging to the WTO. The expected benefits for developing countries (and indeed, most of the recent accessions have been developing countries) include MFN-based [Most Favored Nation] market access with all the other members, the protection of rules against the whims of the powerful, and an enforceable dispute-settlement mechanism to uphold that protection.[33]

In other words, all the hassles and intrusions aside, most countries find participating in a trading world based on rules (even if many of those rules are not to their liking) preferable to existing in one with no rules at all—a world in which a twisted version of the golden rule prevails: "He who has the gold makes the rules."

It is naive to assume, however, that such a rule-free world (WTO rules aside) does not exist. In most cases, realpolitik (a politics based on practical and material factors rather than on theoretical or ethical objectives) prevails. As economist Joseph Stiglitz observes:

> The trade ministries [of WTO Members] reflect the concerns of the business community—both exporters who want to see new markets opened up for their products and producers of goods which fear competition from new imports. These constituencies, of course, want to maintain as many barriers to trade as they can and keep whatever subsidies they can persuade Congress (or their parliament) to give them.[34]

According to *Rachel's Environment & Health Weekly #679*, the WTO isn't mainly about trade. It is mainly about establishing the kind of economy, worldwide, in which the owning class gets to make all important decisions without interference from governments or from anyone else. Today the key institution of the owning class is the corporation, so the aim of the WTO is to ensure that corporations are empowered to make all the important decisions without interference.[35]

Rules, rules, rules! Details, details, details! Some WTO agreements, derived from the various trade rounds, run to thousands of pages. WTO critics may have it wrong when they accuse the organization of being high on free trade. If free trade (beyond trade liberalization) is supposedly the WTO's goal, why, then, are there so many rules about tariffs, subsidy elimination, and quota reductions? Why is there not simply a sentence or two to require members to eliminate all restrictions? In the chapters to come, we will find out why the World Trade Organization—which operates in the real world, where countries constantly seek "concessions" for every tariff reduction they give, even if reducing such tariffs is in their own best interests—finds doing such a "simple" thing impossible.

The Environment
and the WTO

USING THE POLE-AND-LINE METHOD, SPORT FISHERS HAVE FOR decades caught tuna, particularly yellowfin, as the fish swim the warm waters of the eastern tropical Pacific (ETP). It can be a thrilling experience, bringing in a 400-pound tuna after hours of struggle. Catching tuna one fish at a time is no way to make a living from the tasty, meaty giants, however. To catch tons of tuna requires other, more inclusive methods. In the late 1950s, commercial fishers in San Diego, California, took tuna harvesting to a new level with the development of a technology based on the use of synthetic purse-seine netting. As a result, millions of tuna have, over the last half-century, wound up in sandwiches for school kids and salads for their parents. As a by-product of such productive tuna catches, however, millions of dolphins have been killed.

Experts look at the body of a dead dolphin on the beach near the Black Sea town of Shabla, Bulgaria, in May 2006. More than 50 dead dolphins were spotted near Shabla. The government's environmental office believes that the animals died of suffocation after getting entangled in fishing nets.

A seine is a large net that hangs vertically in the water. Along the top edge are floats; along the bottom edge are weights. The net hangs like a fence in the water, ready to be towed into a capturing circle by a boat. In a purse seine, a rope that passes through rings at the bottom of the net is pulled tight to prevent fish from "sounding," or swimming down, to escape the net. (The name comes from the fact that the rope-and-ring arrangement, when pulled in, resembles the closing on an old-fashioned drawstring purse.) When set, purse-seine nets can be up to a mile in circumference.

Tuna fishers have known for some time that their prey swim with dolphins. The dolphin schools swim above the yellowfin tuna. Because the dolphins must come to the surface to breathe, they are easy to spot. Tuna boats simply set nets around schools of dolphins, knowing that tuna will be caught as well. Using speedboats, helicopters, and small explosives, the fishers herd both tuna and dolphins into the encircling purse-seine nets.

As dolphins become entangled in a seine net, they, along with the tuna, die. The animals drown or are crushed. Throughout the 1960s, as many as 250,000 dolphins perished each year because of this form of industrial tuna fishing. It is estimated that 7 million dolphins have died in the ETP as a result of being snarled in purse-seine nets.[36]

In 1972, the United States Congress, in no small part in reaction to the enormous dolphin kill rate, passed the Marine Mammal Protection Act (MMPA). By the end of the 1970s, mainly because of improved technology, dolphin bycatch death rates declined significantly to approximately 20,000 per year.[37]

As U.S. tuna fleets decreased in size over the years, fleets in Latin American countries, particularly in Mexico, picked up the slack. The dolphin bycatch started to rise again. In response, the United States began to require that imported tuna be caught at dolphin mortality rates comparable to those achieved by U.S. fishers.

Mexico was not happy. In 1990, it appealed to the GATT for redress. Mexico claimed that the United States had no right to exclude from its market tuna caught by fishers using purse seines. The United States, Mexico argued, should not be allowed to require standards of conduct outside its borders, even with regard to a product destined for its domestic market. In 1991, the GATT sided with Mexico. It declared that Section 101 (a) (2) of the MMPA, which excluded foreign-caught tuna caught in seine nets, was in violation of GATT rules.

GATTZILLA VERSUS FLIPPER

Fortunately for the dolphins, the 1991 GATT ruling never went into effect. The Dolphin Protection Consumer Information Act that the United States had passed in 1990, mandating standards for the labeling of tuna as "dolphin-safe," still held. Through it, and the subsequent International Dolphin Conservation Act of 1992, fishing fleets were prohibited from chasing, capturing, and setting nets on dolphins if they wanted to sell their end product as dolphin-safe.

Yet, also in 1992, the European Economic Community (EEC), which sought to export prepared tuna processed from fish caught by encirclement, followed Mexico's action and challenged the U.S. law. In 1994, the GATT again ruled against the U.S. dolphin-protection law.

Both rulings, because they came from the GATT, were not automatically enforceable. After the birth, in 1995, of the WTO, with its stronger enforcement mechanisms, Mexico threatened to take its 1991 case (dubbed *GATTzilla versus Flipper* by environmentalists) to the new organization. With that—according to Lori Wallach and Patrick Woodall, in their comprehensive guide to the WTO—"To avoid the political embarrassment of having the WTO order the U.S. to weaken the dolphin protection (or face millions of dollars in trade sanctions), the Clinton administration obtained a reprieve from Mexico and launched a two-year campaign that ultimately resulted in the gutting of the MMPA."[38]

In the GATT/WTO rulings, the argument was made that "like products" could not be discriminated against—not only on the basis of where they were produced, but also on the basis of how they were produced. In other words, tuna was tuna, no matter where or how it was caught.

Environmentalists were furious. The rulings threatened a long list of environmental laws throughout the world that focused on how seafood and other commodities were harvested or manufactured. According to Wallach and Woodall, "Thus under GATT/WTO jurisprudence, unless there is literally dolphin meat in a can of tuna, making it physically different, a can of tuna caught with dolphin-deadly nets must be treated exactly the same as one caught by dolphin-safe methods."[39]

The question is raised, then, as to just what a "dolphin-safe" label indicates today. The U.S. Tuna Federation, which represents such tuna industry giants as StarKist, Chicken of the Sea, and Bumblebee, reports that, at least for its members, a "dolphin-safe" label means that the tuna they purchase and process was not caught by setting nets on dolphins. On New Year's Eve 2002, however, the George W. Bush administration announced that it would allow "dolphin-safe" labels on tuna caught using purse seines.

The GATT/WTO decisions in the dolphin cases have implications beyond environmental concerns. "Dolphin-safe" is one thing, but "people-safe" is quite another. Can a country ban the import of products made with child labor? Perhaps not. After all, if a country cannot discriminate on the basis of how a product is produced, under WTO rules, it may have no recourse in banning it even if the product is made by child labor. The United States, for example, has a federal law that prohibits the sale of products produced with child labor. The law applies only to items made in the United States, however, not to imports.

CAUGHT IN THE GRIP

Fur trapping, the catching of animals for their pelts, is big business, especially in North America, Russia, and parts of Europe. In the United States, more than 4 million wild animals are trapped for the fashion industry every year.[40] In Canada, the number exceeds a million. In the European Union (EU), the figure is as high as 5 million.[41]

Animal trapping systems either kill an animal outright (90 to 95 percent of the time) or hold the creature alive until a trapper arrives (5 to 10 percent of the time). In the latter instances, a steel-jawed leg-hold trap often is used. Such a trap can be so painful that some animals chew off the trapped limb to escape. Some studies have estimated that as many as one in four animals caught in such traps may resort to this terrible solution.[42]

In 1995, the European Union, long concerned with animal welfare issues, prohibited the use of steel-jawed leg-hold traps for hunting 13 fur-bearing animals. The EU then outlawed the importation of pelts from these animals unless the exporting country forbade the use of steel-jawed leg-hold traps or met other humane trapping standards.

Canada complained bitterly about the EU decision. Canadian representatives were quick to point out that such restraining traps are used because there often is no other practical way to catch certain species. The Canadians reminded critics that the EU traps animals using neck snares, box cages, and leg snares. In 1997, James Stone, the first secretary (trade policy) of the Mission of Canada to the EU, told a symposium, "It is legal to use neck snares in France and the UK, but not in Germany; drowning is permitted for wild animals in Germany, France, Belgium, and the Netherlands but not in Finland unless it is done with state authority. Traps with teeth are banned in France and the UK but permitted in Germany."[43] In Canada's eyes, the EU had no consistent policy regarding animal entrapment but displayed, nonetheless, a good deal of hypocrisy.

Soon enough, the United States and Canada came together to threaten a WTO challenge to the EU policy. The North American countries based their warning on a familiar theme: The WTO, they pointed out, prevents discrimination on the basis of how a product is produced (in this case, trapped). Such trapping, the United States and Canada asserted, does not affect the physical characteristics of the product; the "product" remains the same everywhere. Furthermore, the "production process" in question occurs not only within EU jurisdiction, but also in the territories of third world countries as well. In other words, the EU was, through its ban, imposing restrictions on trade. If the EU wanted, it could ban steel-jawed leg-hold traps within its own territory. It could not, however, ban

(continues on page 64)

CLIMATE REFUGEES

Lately, some strange things have been happening in Bangladesh, a poor south Asian country with a population of 147 million people: In the Sundarbans nature reserve, which is home to the largest population of tigers left in the wild, the trees suddenly have begun to die. What is more, they have started to die in a peculiar way: from the top down. The country's leading scientists believe that this is happening because the water of the massive mangrove swamp in which the trees grow is turning from fresh to salty. Water from the sea is beginning to encroach on the water of the swamp. The seawater is doing this because the level of the sea is rising. It is rising, most scientists believe, because of global warming.

In 2004, it was noticed that the tides in the estuaries of the Ganges, Brahmaputra, and Meghna rivers stopped ebbing and flowing. The waters just stayed at high tide. Also in 2004, Dhaka, the capital of Bangladesh, was hit by floods so severe that the ground floors of most buildings were underwater. A catfish was caught in one of the government buildings.

In 2005, Bangladesh had no winter at all. Although many Westerners assume that the entire subcontinent never has any winter—that the weather is always hot and muggy—this is not the case. For Bangladesh to experience no winter is extremely unusual. Clearly, the country was getting hotter.

In the summer of 2007, thousands of fishers in the Bay of Bengal drowned. The seas were particularly rough, and the government issued storm warnings four times in the space of two months. In the past, such warnings normally occurred twice a year. Every warning meant that fishers who stayed at home lost valuable days at sea. In the face of the fourth warning, many fishers simply had to go out. Officially, 1,700 drowned. Many Bangladeshis believe, however, that the actual number may be closer to 10,000. "Was it climate change?" asked Dr. Ainun Nishat, one of the country's leading environmentalists, as reported in the British newspaper *The Independent.* "We don't know. Was it unusual? Yes."*

Most of Bangladesh is a vast delta of alluvial plains—land built up from the soil deposited by rivers running to the sea. This land is barely above sea level, which makes it susceptible to flooding from waterways swollen by increased infiltration by the ocean. If, by the end of the twenty-first century, sea levels were to rise by three feet—a rise already predicted by some scientists—Bangladesh would, it is feared, experience apocalyptic, Atlantis-like conditions.

"A quarter of the country would be submerged," says Henry Chu, reporting in the *Los Angeles Times.* "Dhaka, now in the center of the nation, would sit within 60 miles of the coast, where boats would float over the drowned remnants of countless town squares, markets, houses, and schools. As many as 30 million people would become refugees in their own land, many of them subsistence farmers with nothing to subsist on any longer."**

Plainly, for Bangladesh, global warming is not a far-off problem; it is a clear and present danger.

---

* "Bangladesh: At the Mercy of Climate Change," *The Independent.* February 19, 2007. Available online at *http://www.independent.co.uk/environment/ climate-change/bangladesh-at-the-mercy-of-climate-change-436950.html.*

** Henry Chu, "Global Warming Gains Foothold in Bangladesh," *Los Angeles Times.* February 25, 2007. Available online at *http://www.boston.com/ news/world/asia/articles/2007/02/25/global_warming_gains_foothold_in_ bangladesh/.*

(continued from page 61)
imported pelts from animals caught in such traps outside the EU's dominion.

The threat of a WTO challenge, through a long, drawn-out process, effectively succeeded in halting the EU policy that banned the importation of cruelly trapped animals. Such threats by the WTO to take action, with the possibility of follow-up economic sanctions, are, by themselves, often enough to thwart pro-environmental or humanitarian impulses on the part of individual countries or political unions.

INVASION OF THE LONGHORNED BEETLES

The Asian long horned beetle (ALB) is one nasty bug. About an inch long when fully grown, the showy insect, native to China, is shiny and black with white spots. Its antennae, alternately ringed in black and white, are longer than its body.

What makes this invasive bug so wicked is its voracious appetite for hardwood trees, particularly maple trees. A female ALB chews into a tree's bark and lays eggs. When the eggs hatch, the immature beetles burrow deeper into the tree. When they reach adulthood, the beetles bore their way out of the tree through half-inch-diameter holes. The beetles' home tree is left riddled with holes and fatally oozing sap. The only way to get rid of the ALB menace is to destroy the beetle in its larval stage. To do so calls for cutting down and burning each infested tree.

The Asian long horned beetle first found its way into the United States sometime in the mid-1990s, in wooden packing containers that came from China and Hong Kong. The beetles soon infested trees in Los Angeles, Chicago, and New York, among other places. In New York City, more than 5,700 trees had to be destroyed; in Chicago, 1,500 trees.[44]

On December 17, 1998, the United States Department of Agriculture (USDA) issued a regulation to ban the ALB. The USDA wanted to require that all wood packing material coming from China and Hong Kong be treated by heating and, if

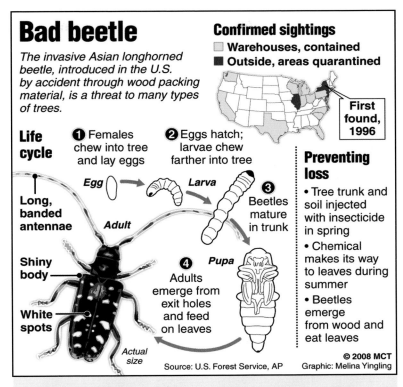

Bad beetle

The invasive Asian longhorned beetle, introduced in the U.S. by accident through wood packing material, is a threat to many types of trees.

Confirmed sightings
- ☐ **Warehouses, contained**
- ■ **Outside, areas quarantined**

First found, 1996

Life cycle

❶ Females chew into tree and lay eggs

❷ Eggs hatch; larvae chew farther into tree

Egg ○ → *Larva*

Long, banded antennae   *Adult*

Shiny body

White spots

❸ Beetles mature in trunk

❹ *Pupa* Adults emerge from exit holes and feed on leaves

Preventing loss
- Tree trunk and soil injected with insecticide in spring
- Chemical makes its way to leaves during summer
- Beetles emerge from wood and eat leaves

Actual size

Source: U.S. Forest Service, AP

© 2008 MCT
Graphic: Melina Yingling

The Asian longhorned beetle has destroyed more than 30,000 U.S. trees since it was first found in 1996. It is brought through untreated wood packing material used to ship imported goods from China. After the United States imposed regulations to stop the beetle, Hong Kong charged that the new safeguards were an illegal trade barrier and threatened to file suit with the WTO.

necessary, fumigation, to insure that no ALB larvae survived to enter the United States.

Hong Kong objected and, as a WTO member, was empowered to take its grievance to the international trade organization. (China was miffed, too; but as it did not become a member of the WTO until 2001, it could not, at the time, bring a case to the trade body.)

Hong Kong claimed that the standards for irradiation (heating) set forth by the United States were too strict and expensive. Hong Kong said that the U.S. requirements lacked the scientific evidence needed to support such actions. Hong Kong further asserted that the United States was just being protectionist, using USDA regulations to thwart Chinese imports.

Once again, the mere threat of a WTO challenge caused a regulating country (in this case, the United States) to pause and reconsider its policy. The United States agreed to let the International Plant Protection Convention (IPPC), a treaty enacted in 1952 to set international standards regarding pest control, lead the way toward a new, anti-invasive species standard. IPPC criteria are presumed to be WTO legal. Thus, in agreeing to work with the IPPC, the United States also was acquiescing in a major goal of the WTO—the goal of harmonizing.

The idea behind harmonization is to replace the various national product standards with one global standard. Because such harmonizing standards, in the eyes of the WTO, serve as ceilings that countries cannot exceed rather than floors that they all must meet, the adaptation of such standards tends to lower the best existing domestic environmental standards. The result, as Lori Wallach and Patrick Woodall claim, is "a one-way downward ratchet on domestic standards—the race-to-the-bottom effect."[45]

WIN-WIN SCENARIOS

The heart of the environmentalists' criticism of the WTO is the organization's understanding that like products cannot be treated differently according to the ways they are produced or harvested. This issue is sure to remain a strong bone of contention with environmentalists long into the future. That antagonism aside, however, there are those in both the WTO and in various environmental organizations who believe that positive links exist between trade liberalization and improvement of the environment, and that such connections should be exploited.

These believers claim that market forces can, at times, work for both the economy and the environment simultaneously, rather than always working for one at the expense of the other.

Fundamental to the above proposition is the belief that trade restrictions are the problem, and that in their liberalization lies the solution. As Gary P. Sampson writes, "Trade restrictions can distort the optimal functioning of markets and thus the exploitation of comparative advantage, just as they can frustrate the implementation of sound environmental management policies."[46] Those who declare that there is a positive link between trade liberalization and environmental improvement believe that many examples of win-win scenarios exist—scenarios in which the elimination of trade restrictions actually improves environmental sustainability.

Fisheries offer one example. Government fishery subsidies (a sum of money granted by the government to a private person or company to benefit the public) that make it less costly to exploit fisheries lead to overfishing and thus to depleted fish stocks. If the government subsidies are eliminated, the argument goes, it will cost more to fish, fewer fish will be caught, and fish stocks will reach more sustainable levels.

The same link is said to exist for agriculture. Trade-distorting agricultural export subsidies in developed countries depress world prices. As a consequence, it is said, poor farmers in developing countries cannot compete. In an attempt to grow more crops, the poor farmers are forced to cultivate marginal lands that are subject to erosion and runoff and are moved to clear forests for agricultural use. These practices obviously are bad for the environment.

Links between subsidies and environmental degradation also can exist with regard to energy. Among other things, such subsidies often encourage obsolete and environmentally inefficient energy technologies to continue to operate.

Central to a belief in a win-win scenario to which trade liberalization is the key is the issue of trade in environmental goods and services. The value of pollution-control and solid-waste management products and services is estimated at more than $450 billion per year. As Sampson points out, "In this sector, as in others, it is in the interest of all WTO members that environmentally sound goods and services be made available on the international market at the cheapest prevailing world prices."[47]

In the final analysis, those who support the link between freer trade (with its resulting growth) and environmental sustainability rest their case most persuasively on the belief that in such a world, there will be more resources available to protect the environment. It is rich countries, the argument goes, that can best afford to seek environmental sustainability. The sooner poor countries become rich, or richer, the better off the world, and its environment, will be.

Workers of the World and the WTO

IN THE HUANYA GIFTS FACTORY, CHRISTMAS TREE ORNAMENTS are made for retail giant Wal-Mart. The factory is located in Guangzhou, China, a huge, gritty industrial city 75 miles northwest of Hong Kong. It is to Huanya that brothers Xu Wenquan (age 16) and Xu Wenjie (age 18) went to look for work in late 2007, having journeyed over 500 miles from impoverished Guizhou Province. "I work on the plastic molding machine from six in the morning to six at night," Xu Wenquan told *New York Times* reporter David Barboza. The machines are "quite hot, so I've burned my hands." Xu's hands were covered with blisters.[48] When Chinese government inspectors visited Huanya, the two young brothers were given a day off.

A former employee gave Barboza a similar account of what amounted to a sweatshop environment—a workplace in which employees work under dreadful conditions—at Huanya. "It's quite noisy, and you stand up all day, 12 hours, and there's no air-conditioning," he told Barboza, as reported in the *Times* article above. "We get paid by the piece we make but they never told us how much. Sometimes I got $110, sometimes I got $150 a month."

Factories such as Huanya have been accused of routinely shortchanging their employees; exposing their workers to dangerous machinery and harmful chemicals (among them lead, cadmium, and mercury); and withholding health benefits. According to a study published by the Shanghai Academy of Social Sciences, factory workers in and around Guangzhou lose or break about 40,000 fingers on the job each year.[49]

Darin Sisoipha (age 15) also has experienced physical abuse in her work at a factory in Bangkok, Thailand. There, she labors for nine hours a day, six days a week, for $2 per day. "Twice the needles went right through her hands," the girl's mother, Maesubin Sisoipha, told *New York Times* reporter Nicholas Kristof. "But the managers bandaged up her hands, and both times she got better again and went back to work."[50]

Maesubin Sisoipha's comment may strike many as callous, but this mother was not indifferent to her daughter's suffering. Quite simply, this family's take on a sweatshop job is entirely different from that of most Westerners. "It's good pay," a friend, Mongkol Latlakorn, told Kristof. "I hope she can keep that job. There's all this talk about factories closing. . . . I don't know what she would do then."

Clearly, what some see as exploitation, others see as opportunity.

As grim as many southern Chinese factories are, they have contributed to a remarkable explosion of wealth among that country's 1.2 billion people. In Dongguan Province, wages have gone from $50 per month to more than $250 per month in less than a decade.[51] There, as elsewhere, workers seek out factories that allow employees to toil seven days a week, regardless of the grueling workload. More time at work means more income.

Such is the situation throughout much of Asia and in many other parts of the developing world. For many poor countries, particularly those at or near the very bottom of the economic ladder (Cambodia and Bangladesh come quickly to mind), the only things they have to offer the world are workers who are willing to toil for dirt-cheap wages. It is their one comparative advantage—at least for now.

Although sweatshops can and must be improved, for many poor countries and their workers, they are, quite simply, the price paid for development. Had Taiwan and South Korea not allowed for sweatshops decades ago (the argument goes), these two East Asian countries might never have achieved their phenomenal economic success.

NIKE ON THE RUN

Nike—the shoe manufacturer with the "Swoosh" logo that is recognized around the world—employs about 500,000 workers in 51 countries, many in Southeast Asia. In 1989, the company paid its lead celebrity spokesperson, basketball superstar Michael Jordan, more money—$25 million—than the 25,000 workers in the entire Indonesian shoe industry made in combined wages.[52]

In the 1990s, people around the world, but particularly in developed countries such as the United States, began to protest this seeming economic disparity. Critics wanted working conditions to be improved at Nike plants everywhere. Protesters demanded that Nike make commitments to raise the minimum age for their factory workers, to expand worker education, to increase factory monitoring, and to ensure that their factories met standards for indoor air quality set by the U.S. Occupational Safety and Health Administration (OSHA).

Supporters and detractors of globalization have been at odds about American companies with factories in underdeveloped countries. Some activists oppose these factories saying that they pay miniscule wages while reaping enormous profits at the expense of workers. Economists point out that those wages, though small by U.S. standards, are in fact high in a third-world country. *Above,* workers at a Nike factory on the outskirts of Ho Chi Minh City, Vietnam, assemble shoes.

Nike agreed to implement the previously named improvements but balked when it came to raising wages, eliminating forced overtime, and granting broader worker rights. At the heart of the matter was the issue of comparative advantage. Nike was making shoes in Southeast Asia rather than in the United States for a reason: lower costs.

Sarah Bachman summed up the matter best in *YaleGlobal* (the online magazine of the Yale Center for the Study of Globalization) when she asked, on June 27, 2003:

What is a 'sweatshop' after all? Should third-world factories, where people are evidently happy for factory jobs making products for export and often are paid more than workers in an economy's domestic sector, have the same worker safety and pay standards as in U.S. or European workplaces? Don't lower safety and pay standards serve developing countries by making them more competitive, and thus more able to work their way out of poverty? Are anti-sweatshop protests merely a smokescreen for protectionism?[53]

Enter the World Trade Organization.

Many of the protesters at the WTO's Seattle Ministerial Meeting in 1999 demanded, among other things, that the trade organization address the issue of dismal labor standards in developing countries. The WTO's response was a familiar one. As has been seen, the WTO strongly discourages nations from excluding imported goods because of the way those goods are produced.

The WTO's antidiscrimination principles notwithstanding, the organization attempts to address low worker standards around the world in a more fundamental way. The WTO believes that freer trade leads to economic growth. Growth, in turn, will be followed by increased incentives to raise worker wages and working conditions. In other words, the WTO insists that freeing up market forces, through trade liberalization, to do their "magic", is the answer to the eventual elimination of sweatshop working conditions around the world.

TWO THOUSAND BRICKS A DAY

To let adults work long hours, under harsh conditions, with minimal health and safety provisions, all for subsistence wages, is one thing. To force children, many of them under 16 and some as young as 5, to do so is quite another. It happens, however. Officially, 320 million children work worldwide, often under incredible stress, both physical and mental.[54]

According to Dr. David Parker, an occupational physician and the author of the book *Before Their Time: The World of Child Labor*, the following accounts are typical:

> Throughout much of the world, bricks are made by hand. In Asia, Latin America, and Africa, children and adults dig clay for bricks using shovels, picks, and awls. . . . When the bricks are dry, barefoot workers load them on their backs or on top of their heads and carry them across fields of stones and broken bricks. Each brick weighs four to nine pounds. A small child may haul 1,000 to 2,000 bricks each day. . . .
>
> In India, Pakistan, Turkey, and other countries, children knot wool or silk carpets. Children who spend day after day doing this type of detailed handwork are likely to develop arthritis at an early age. Virtually all children who knot carpets get skin rashes and frequently cut their hands with razors or knives. . . .
>
> Children tan leather in cottage industries around the world. Leather tanning is one of the dirtiest jobs imaginable, carried out in a tumbling barrel or large vats using chromic acid, oxalic acid, formaldehyde, and alkalis such as trisodium phosphate and borax. In addition to exposing workers to toxic chemicals, the process releases carbon monoxide, hydrogen sulfide, and other noxious gases.[55]

So disgusting is the tanning industry, even China is fed up with it. As a consequence, the Asian giant is seeking to export what little it has left of tanning to countries such as Bangladesh.

There are, of course, international laws and treaties that attempt to regulate or eliminate child labor. Since the Universal Declaration of Human Rights was adopted by the United Nations in 1948, dozens of international treaties concerning children's rights have been written.

Three young participants in the Global March Against Child Labor hold a banner after arriving at the 1998 International Labor Organization Conference in Geneva, Switzerland. The march, which included thousands of people, not only brought awareness to the problem of child labor and the need for education for all children, it also helped the revision of Convention No. 182 get passed, the decree that became the guideline for governments when creating labor laws.

Yet, clearly, more needs to be done.

In May 2008, Chinese officials broke up a child-labor ring that forced children from poor inland areas to work in booming coastal cities. "Most of the work force comes from underdeveloped or poverty-stricken areas," said Hu Xingdou, a professor of economics and social policy at the Beijing Institute of Technology, as reported by David Barboza in the *New York Times*. "Some children are even sold by their parents, who often don't have any idea of the working conditions."[56]

The WTO does not, of course, condone child labor. Yet, given the WTO's nondiscrimination principle, it is perhaps fair to ask whether a country can prohibit the importation of products made by child labor. Would such a prohibition not discriminate against a product on the basis of how it is manufactured?

CORPORATE GIANTS

Multinational corporations are at the center of today's world economy and thus of world trade. Some of these worldwide corporations are richer than most countries. In 2005, Wal-Mart, with revenues of $285 billion, outdid the combined gross domestic product (GDP; the total market value of the goods and services that a country or countries produce in a specific period) of all of sub-Saharan Africa.[57]

Such corporations, according to critics, spread their tentacles everywhere and often answer only to themselves; they seek profits by cutting costs through holding wages down, often to starvation levels. In the developed world, when wage demands become too aggressive, multinationals are quick to prove just how global they are: They send jobs offshore by the thousands or simply pack up and leave for greener (cheaper) pastures. It is said that multinationals pollute wherever they go; bribe whenever necessary; care only for the bottom line; and, by doing so, make outrageous profits. As one argument goes, multinationals live to trade and—through their "puppet," the WTO—see to it that ever-freer trade (their own industries' protectionist demands notwithstanding) dominate economic agendas everywhere.

Yet, as Joseph Stiglitz, no corporate lackey, is quick to concede, "Corporations have been at the center of helping to raise standards of living throughout much of the world. . . . Corporations have brought jobs and economic growth to the developing nations, and inexpensive goods of increasingly high quality to the developed ones, lowering the cost of living and so contributing to an era of low inflation and low interest rates."[58]

Good, bad, or both, multinational corporations are here to stay. Indeed, new ones are popping up in some unlikely places. Long identified with the West and with developed countries, homegrown, giant multinationals recently have sprung up in countries such as Brazil, India, and China, ready to compete with the likes of Cisco Systems, Boeing, IBM, and Sony.

The emerging multinationals represent both an opportunity and a threat to workers worldwide. "These companies are hiring people from anywhere in the world," says economist Peter J. Williamson, as reported by William J. Holstein in the *New York Times*. "A lot of people who felt that their companies or their jobs were protected because they were in the high-value-added or high-tech kinds of businesses used to think that the rise of these companies was irrelevant to them. . . . But now they are going to find they are under significant competition from these companies."[59]

Can the United States compete in this new world economic reality, a world that seems to make while Americans take? Contrary to public perception, the answer is a cautionary yes.

Believe it or not, the United States still makes stuff—lots of stuff. Today, the United States is the world's largest manufacturer. America has never exported more, both in terms of dollars ($1.6 trillion in 2007) and as a percentage of GDP (11.8 percent). True, the United States imports even more than it exports. As Justin Fox, writing in *Time* magazine, puts it, "The United States has continued to run surpluses in some high-tech, high-price-tag categories—aircraft, specialized industrial machines—and in agricultural commodities. It's in consumer goods—clothing, TVs, cars—that the big deficits show up."[60]

Of course, although trade benefits an economy as a whole, some workers, especially at the bottom, will be displaced. According to *The Economist*, "When a country with relatively more high-skilled workers (such as America) trades with poorer countries that have relatively more low-skilled workers, America's low skilled will lose out."[61] There are many who argue that it is, in part, the WTO's job to help moderate what is a difficult adjustment for many workers or, more importantly, to insist on some kind of linkage between universal labor standards and trade. The WTO, however, has been reluctant to establish such a connection.

THE WTO AND THE SOCIAL CLAUSE

Interestingly, even before the WTO came into existence, there was talk of just such a linkage in the form of a so-called "social clause." In 1994, the year before the WTO's founding, France and the United States suggested that a social clause advocating international labor standards be included in the charter for the WTO. According to Wallach and Woodall,

> The Social Clause concept would allow importing countries to take trade measures against exporting countries that failed to enforce core labor standards with punitive actions ranging from reduced quotas or raised tariffs to complete embargoes on all imports from the country in question. . . . While such a policy would not inherently raise wages in poorer countries, it would eliminate corporate profit incentives to deny the labor rights necessary for workers to fight for improvements. The bottom line would be altered: If a product cannot be sold in the desired market, it does not matter how cheaply it can be produced.[62]

In determining what such a social clause would consist of, proponents suggested that the WTO needed to look no further than action taken by the International Labor Organization (ILO) in establishing four core labor rights principles:

1. the elimination of all forms of forced or compulsory labor

THE PRISONERS' DILEMMA

As they seek a comparative advantage by providing low-cost manu-facturing opportunities to multinational corporations, poor coun-tries strive to outdo each other in what many observers see as a race to the bottom. Such countries do not set out to see their workers paid a pittance, receive little in the way of benefits, or suc-cumb to health and safety calamities. Uncertain as to how compet-ing countries will act, however, an undeveloped country, with little else to offer, may keep lowering the bar in order to gain or main-tain a comparative advantage.

The solution to this predicament—a solution whereby wages and working conditions for all workers at the bottom would rise—is for various countries to cooperate in demanding higher standards from multinational corporations. For that to occur, how-ever, all, or nearly all, of the cooperating countries would have to understand where the others stood and work together to achieve a common goal. All would have to agree to abide by the new stan-dards and to not give in when a multinational attempted to pick off a country by providing work at lower standards for its nationals. In other words, countries would have to trust each other not to cheat, not to break the deal, and not to seek a temporary com-parative advantage.

Failure to achieve cooperation can, perhaps, best be under-stood in reference to the classic problem called "the prisoners' dilemma," which seeks to illustrate the tension between coopera-tion and competition.

In the traditional version of the social scientists' prisoners' dilemma game, the police have arrested two suspects and are interrogating them separately. Each suspect can keep silent, or one

(continues)

(continued)

can confess and thereby incriminate the other. Each suspect, regardless of what the other does, can improve his or her position by confessing. When both confess, however, the outcome is worse for both suspects than it is when both keep silent. The dominant strategy is for each to confess. This is too bad, because if both suspects trusted each other to cooperate, and neither confessed, both would escape punishment. "However," Wallach and Woodall point out, in *Whose Trade Organization?*, "each prisoner experiences strong temptation to betray the other and thus be punished only slightly, out of fear of *being* betrayed and suffering severe punishment."

So it is with developing countries. As Wallach and Woodall continue, "Developing-world countries, desperate for investment and creation of jobs and lacking information about each other's choices and motives, opt for bad bargains out of fear that their neighbors cannot be trusted to transact with common interests in mind."

Clearly, as long as solidarity among developing countries on matters of working conditions is lacking, a divide-and-conquer pattern will allow multinational corporations to keep calling the shots. Only cooperation and trust can break the cycle.

2. the elimination of discrimination in respect to employment and occupation
3. freedom of association and the effective recognition of the right to collective bargaining
4. the effective abolition of child labor.

As commendable as these principles are, the ILO was (and is) an international body with weak enforcement capacity and was unable to do much to insist that such principles be carried out. The WTO, on the other hand, can enforce trade sanctions on rule violators. Why not (the argument went) have the WTO adopt and enforce the ILO's principles?

Opposition came from a number of sources, including many developing countries.

The opposition's first concern was, and still is, that any such labor standards and trade linkages are, in fact, nothing but ill-disguised protectionism. Such standards, some critics felt, were a neocolonial encroachment on countries' national sovereignty. In other words, the cry by developed countries to see labor standards rise in developing countries is motivated more by self-interest than by any altruism on the developed countries' parts.

A more significant reason to oppose a forced raising of labor standards through the WTO was perhaps best expressed by developing country representatives at the WTO's first ministerial meeting, in Singapore, in 1996. There, the representatives stated: "[We] reject the use of labor standards for protectionist purposes, and agree that the comparative advantage of countries, particularly low-wage developing countries, must in no way be put into question."[63]

Thus, with resistance from the very countries for which higher labor standards are designed to provide uplift, the prospect of the WTO's adopting a social clause any time soon seems remote, indeed.

Public Safety
and the WTO

BARRY BONDS, THE FORMER SAN FRANCISCO GIANTS HOME-run king, may or may not have used steroids to pump up his muscle mass. When it comes to U.S. cattle, however, there is no argument: The vast majority are injected with drugs, particularly anabolic steroids, to make them lean, strong, and, well, beefier.

The meat of these hormone-treated bovines has been gracing American dinner tables for decades. Beef producers administer a host of synthetic hormones by inserting a slow-release pellet into a steer's ear. Because ears become by-products and so are not processed as meat for human consumption, local concentrations of the hormone do not wind up in people's food. Furthermore, the USDA requires that the synthetic hormones be withdrawn before the animals are slaughtered. "The regulatory goal is to ensure that anyone eating beef will get a dose of residual hormones that's less than one percent of the highest dose that caused no ill effect in test animals," says Susan Brewer, associate professor of food chemistry at the University of Illinois at Champaign. "We have a 100-fold safety factor built into the tolerances."[64]

Although consumers in the United States may consider steroid-pumped beef safe for consumption, the European Union does not. In 1988, the EU banned the sale of beef (grown domestically or in foreign countries) from cattle treated with any of six artificial hormones that are linked to cancer and to premature pubescence (very early puberty) in girls. In doing this, the EU adopted what is known as a "zero risk" standard. This means that, although the health risk from hormone-treated beef is uncertain, the EU was not going to take any chances. Besides, the argument went, as Europeans simply did not want to eat such beef, why offer it for sale? All such beef was to be banned.

In 1996, the United States, acting at the request of the U.S.-based National Cattlemen's Association, challenged the EU policy at the WTO. A year later, the WTO ruled against the European Union. The WTO ruling said, in part, that hormones in beef had not been scientifically proven to be dangerous to humans. In 1998, the WTO ordered the EU either to begin importing artificial hormone-treated beef from the United States by May 13, 1999, or to conduct a WTO-legal (high standard) risk assessment to justify not doing so.

In this case, the WTO was saying that the EU must base any assessment of risk on international standards, or, if the EU's standards departed from international standards, the EU standards must be based on an extensive risk assessment. If, after the risk assessment, no health hazard was found to exist, the EU must remove what the United States and other beef-exporting countries were claiming was an unfair barrier to trade.

The EU attempted to conduct such a risk assessment in answer to the WTO ruling. The results did not satisfy the WTO, however. In response, the WTO authorized the United States to impose $116.8 million worth of trade sanctions against European-made products. As a penalty for not accepting American hormone-raised beef (a loss to the American cattle industry of about $500 million annually), European Union products such as truffles, mustards, and cheeses would not be allowed to cross the Atlantic for U.S. consumption.[65]

The $116.8 million per year in sanctions that the EU suffers is a price most Europeans seem willing to pay for keeping a product they do not want off their dinner tables. Interestingly, as Wallach and Woodall's book is quick to point out, "This is the only WTO ruling—with two wealthy nations [the United States and the EU as a whole], each of whom can afford continuing WTO litigation and bear sanctions—that has resulted in such an outcome rather than the losing country changing its policy."[66]

TRADE BARRIERS VERSUS PUBLIC HEALTH

One of the first agreements signed when the WTO came into existence has turned out, arguably, to be the WTO's most controversial agreement. Known as the Sanitary and Phytosanitary Agreement, or SPS, it is designed to deal with health threats from plant-borne organisms. More generally, the SPS is supposed to ensure a government's right to protect its citizens' food sources, both plant and animal.

According to the WTO Web site, the agreement was formulated "to maintain the sovereign right of any government to provide the level of health protection it deems appropriate." The Web site, referring to a government inquiry, poses a simple question: "How do you ensure that your country's consumers are being supplied with food that is safe to eat—'safe' by the standards you consider appropriate?" The Web site then goes on to ask a follow-up question, one that has served to ignite international quarrels: "And at the same time, how can you

A cook prepares imported U.S. beef at a store in Seoul, Korea, in July 2007. For the first time in four years, the country resumed limited imports of U.S. beef, amid public protest. In 2003, the country closed what was then the third-largest market for U.S. beef exporters due to concerns of mad cow disease. As of October 2008, the WTO's top court backed the United States and Canada in their suit against Europe's long-standing ban on beef treated with growth hormones.

ensure that strict health and safety regulations are not being used as an excuse for protecting domestic producers?"[67]

For the WTO—which always is keen to remind everyone that WTO agreements are negotiated by member governments and therefore reflect those governments' concerns—the bottom line is clear: Do not use safety as an excuse to limit imports and thus protect domestic producers. This bottom line is to be true even if domestic products are subject to the same health standards (nondiscrimination) as foreign products seeking entrance.

As has been shown, the EU controversy regarding the importation of U.S. beef illustrates the tension the SPS

Agreement engenders. Is American hormone-fed beef really unsafe for human consumption, or is halting its import just a protectionist excuse? Is James Marsden, a former chief scientist of the American Meat Institute, right when he argues that over-supply of beef on the continent is the real issue? "I've lost any confidence that any science is driving this," he has said. "It's a convenient way to prevent competition."[68]

Critics of the WTO's SPS Agreement become most vocal when they point out that the agreement, in their minds, turns the common-sense precautionary principle on its head. That principle, which is claimed to be an established pillar of public policy everywhere, says that when suspicion exists as to the safety of a substance or process, it is better to err on the side of caution. In other words, when in doubt, play it safe: Restrict.

Detractors claim, however, that under the WTO SPS Agreement, one must prove that a substance is dangerous before one can restrict its use. According to the Web site "What's Wrong with the WTO?", "The WTO assumes untested chemicals and technologies are safe until proven otherwise. This stands the Precautionary Principle—better safe than sorry—on its head, and can force nations to lower their public health, safety, and environmental standards."[69]

As was shown in the EU beef case, the WTO requires "sci-entifically supported" risk assessment before countries can jus-tifiably restrict what they claim are dangerous imports. Critics maintain, however, that as the WTO establishes standards for risk assessment, it does not set floors on safety provisions, thereby allowing nations and localities to set higher levels of safety and protection. Instead, the WTO actually does the reverse. It sets ceilings that can be used to strike down any pro-tections that exceed them.

TOXIC TEETHING RINGS

When babies and small children put things other than food in their mouths, there is always cause for concern. Small objects such as fasteners, toy parts, and the like are to be avoided at all costs. But teethers? Teethers are designed to be placed in a baby's mouth. Infants gnaw on teething rings to ease their aching gums, to provide some relief to the pain that is caused as growing teeth stretch and then break through those tender baby gums.

A good teething ring should be pliable, not brittle. To make hard plastic (the substance from which most teething rings are made) softer, certain chemical additives are mixed in with the plastic as it is formed in a mold. The result is a pleasingly chewable object.

Such rings have failed to calm parents, however—at least many parents who live in the European Union. Worried about potentially toxic substances called phthalates that were used to make teething rings spongier, in 1997 the EU moved to regulate toxic substances placed in teethers and other toys that might be put in the mouth. American toy manufacturers were not amused. They were quick to suggest that the EU's proposal might be an illegal barrier to trade and suggested that a WTO challenge might be in order. According to a U.S. State Department memo, "Leading toy manufacturers contacted the Commerce Department . . . to rectify the problem."[70]

The United States, of course, had its own standards when it came to limiting phthalates in toys. The State Department informed its European station chiefs that the Toy Manufacturers of America voluntarily limited such phthalates to 3 percent in pacifiers and teethers. The United States told European countries that American standards were high enough and that any attempt on their part to raise standards further was not only unnecessary, but also a hindrance to free trade.

The State Department urged its European embassies to press for the elimination of the EU ban on phthalates. In doing this, America's Clinton administration went to bat for Mattel and other United States–based toy manufacturers. The Europeans refused to be intimidated, however. They

Kids Health Matters

Toxic toys

Did you ever think those cute rubber duckies could harm your baby? Studies show some toys can be dangerous.

What's the worry?

■ PVC (polyvinyl chloride) plastic: Brittle material to which toy-makers add softeners, called phthalates, to make it flexible

■ Phthalates can leak from PVC when kids chew on toy

■ Animal tests show that phthalates damage liver, kidneys and reproductive system

Phthalates

PVC

What parents can do

■ Avoid buying PVC toys; choose ones from companies that label toys PVC-free

■ Call manufacturers' toll-free numbers to find out what materials are used in toys

■ Demand better product labeling; makers are not required to label all materials used in toys

© 2001 KRT
Source: Greenpeace
Graphic: Pat Carr, Laura Pearl

Phthalates are additives used in a variety of products, including nail polish, caulk, and children's toys. In 2004, a Swedish-Danish research team found a strong link between allergies in children and the phthalates DEHP and BBzP. Several countries have banned phthalates from children's toys, and some phthalates will be restricted in the U.S. state of California.

decided simply to let individual nations regulate phthalates on a country-by-country basis.

In a *Wall Street Journal* article dated November 12, 1998, and entitled "Toy Makers Say Bye-Bye to 'Plasticizers,'" it was announced that the U.S. toy industry would begin phasing out phthalates from products designed to be placed in the mouths of babies.

The teething-ring controversy is one of only a few cases in which the threat of taking it to the WTO backfired. Critics maintain that in the vast majority of situations, especially when a threatened country lacks the knowledge and resources to fight back, that sort of bullying works, and some sort of "accommodation" is reached before the WTO is "forced" to take action.

UP IN SMOKE

In 2001, in response to a cigarette labeling regulatory proposal by Canada, American tobacco giant Philip Morris was quick to disclaim any health benefits to its "light" or "ultra-light" cigarettes. The company agreed that "consumers should not be given the message that descriptors mean that any brand of cigarettes has been shown to be less harmful than other brands."[71] Philip Morris did contend, however, that such words communicated a difference in taste. In view of this, Philip Morris asserted, the use of the terms *light* and *ultra-light* was harmless. In consequence, the company concluded, it had every right to print the descriptors on its cigarette packages as part of its tobacco trademark.

Earlier, the Canadian government had insisted that the descriptors *mild* and *light* were fundamentally misleading. The government cited data that suggested that more than a third of the people who purchased "light" or "mild" cigarettes did so for health reasons, believing that such cigarettes were less harmful than "regular" brands. In reality, the data showed, these types of cigarettes are not less harmful, in part because smokers compensate for the cigarettes' lower tar and nicotine levels by inhaling more deeply. Canada wanted the "mild" and "light" labels removed from cigarettes sold within its borders.

In response to Canada's threat to regulate tobacco labeling, Philip Morris claimed that such regulations would violate a basic WTO rule by "encumbering the use and function of valuable, well-known tobacco trademarks."[72] Even more importantly, according to the tobacco company, Canada would be in violation of a key WTO agreement, an actual treaty known as the Agreement on Technical Barriers to Trade (TBT). A violation of the WTO's TBT was to be considered a serious matter.

The objective of the TBT agreement is to ensure that technical negotiations and standards, as well as testing and certification procedures, do not create unnecessary obstacles to trade. The TBT agreement requires that governments, as they seek to regulate matters such as health, choose the least trade-restrictive means of pursuing their objectives. The WTO wants to make sure that governments do not lay down mandatory technical regulations in a protectionist attempt to limit trade.

Specifically, the TBT agreement insists that:

1. Any regulations must not be more trade restrictive than what is necessary to fulfill a legitimate objective.
2. The risks involved in not having a regulation will need to be weighted against the effects on trade, to determine whether the regulations are disproportionate in light of the risks.
3. The assessment of the risks must be based on rational considerations, such as scientific information.[73]

Philip Morris argued that the WTO's TBT agreement was being violated in the Canadian case because less restrictive means exist to ensure that consumers are not mislead into believing that there are any health benefits to "light" and "mild" tobacco products. The company claimed, for example, that it simply could have been required to state on a cigarette package that the term *light* does not mean that the product has been shown to be safer than other cigarettes.

Philip Morris never pressured the United States government to take its case to the WTO, probably because the company feared negative publicity. Tobacco-control advocates fear, however, that other national governments, less able to withstand pressure from big tobacco, will cave in and refuse to seek such labeling protection. Thus, in critics' eyes, this is another example of a mere threat to take a matter to the WTO being sufficient to dampen any action by a government to set higher health standards.

HARMONIZATION

The central goal of the WTO—indeed, its key mandate—is to promote freer trade everywhere, and to do so by reducing tariff and nontariff barriers, in addition to minimizing regulations and standards that, in the mind of the WTO, restrict the free flow of goods and services. The organization's job is to promote a worldwide market economy in which government regulation is kept to a minimum.

Governments, however, as they attempt to fulfill their mandate to promote the general welfare, do impose restrictions, regulations, and standards that relate to a host of items and processes. In the eyes of the WTO, such domestic rules and regulations pose a problem in that they are not only numerous and varied, but also often arbitrary and unbacked by sound science. To correct these problems, the WTO seeks to harmonize standards; that is, to promote international standards that all its members must agree to. In other words, the WTO seeks global standardization.

For the WTO, harmonization is based on the idea that the world is one huge market. Rather than allow for individual national standards, which (in the view of the WTO) are undesirable because they fragment global markets, the WTO wants universal standards. The WTO wants such harmonized standards even if standards that vary from country to country reflect differences in cultures and values. This is true even if national standards provide a greater level of consumer protection than harmonized, universal standards would.

PIG GUTS AND BAD DRUGS

Heparin is a hugely popular blood thinner that is used around the world in surgery and dialysis (a machine-aided blood-cleansing method used in patients whose kidneys have failed). In 2007, the U.S. Food and Drug Administration (FDA) linked 19 deaths and hundreds of severe allergic reactions to the use of heparin. The heparin in question came from China and contained a chemically modified substance that mimicked the real drug. Although it is yet to be determined that the contaminant actually caused the problem, it seems likely that there is a link. Because this situation came on the heels of a pet-food scare in which hundreds, if not thousands, of pets died or were sickened in the United States by Chinese pet-food ingredients that contained deadly levels of a chemical substance called melamine, Americans had cause for concern.

In China, raw material for heparin comes from mucous membranes in the intestines of slaughtered pigs. Once they are harvested, these pig guts are mixed together and cooked. In many parts of China, this process takes place on stove tops in unregulated family workshops.

After this brew is cooked, it is transported to plants that process the active ingredients of heparin for shipment to a finished dose manufacturer. There can be many steps from the slaughter of the pigs to the final pharmaceutical. Much can go wrong along this extended supply chain, especially as inspection and regulation often fall short.

Of course, as one sets such harmonized international standards, the question arises as to just what level of standardization is to be sought. Critics of harmonization maintain that the strived-for WTO standards always will be the lowest possible—the better to encourage the freest flow of goods and services. As Wallach and Woodall point out:

According to investigative journalist Walt Bogdanich, writing in the *New York Times*, "After many near misses and warning signs, the heparin scare has eliminated any doubt that, here and abroad, regulatory agencies overseeing the safety of medicine are overwhelmed in a global economy where supply chains are long and opaque, and often involve many manufacturers."

Central to the problem are the opportunities for counterfeiting and adulterating drug products. "Advanced technology and global manufacturing outlets have made fake drugs a big and illicit business that is literally poisoning patients," Alan C. Drewsen (executive director of the International Trademark Association) told Bogdanich. "The World Health Organization runs a program that helps track counterfeit medicine, but it has no regulatory authority," Bogdanich wrote.

"In the 1990s governments were all about trying to maximize the volume of international trade," Moisés Naím (editor in chief of *Foreign Policy* magazine and author of *Illicit: How Smugglers, Traffickers and Copycats Are Hijacking the Global Economy*) told the *Times*. "I'm all for that, but I believe this decade is going to be about maximizing the quality of that trade, not quantity."

Walt Bogdanich. "The Drug Scare That Exposed a World of Hurt," *New York Times*. March 30, 2008, The World, 3.

Theoretically, international harmonization could occur at the lowest or highest levels of public health or environmental protection. Unfortunately, the actual WTO harmonization provisions promote lowering of the best existing domestic public-health, food-safety, plant- and animal-protection and environmental standards around the world. This is the case because, under the WTO, international standards serve as a ceiling which countries cannot exceed, rather than as a floor all countries must meet.[74]

Certainly, the WTO doesn't see it quite that way. Its Web site tells readers that "It allows countries to set their own standards." It says that even though it encourages members to use international standards, "Members may use measures which result in higher standards." To be sure, the WTO then quickly points out that such standards must be based on scientific justification. The WTO, its Web site clarifies, even allows for application of the "safety first" precautionary principle, but only on a temporary basis.[75]

No matter what level of harmonization is achieved, for the WTO the bottom line is always there: Take restrictions down to their lowest level to facilitate the freest possible trade in all commodities and services. If harmonization does not do that, the WTO's market-based philosophy still must prevail, even when countries seek bilateral trade agreements. The WTO Web site states, "If an exporting country can demonstrate that the measures it applies to its exports achieve the same level of health protection as in the importing country, then the importing country is expected to accept the exporting country's standards and methods."[76]

Intellectual Property Rights and the WTO

IT HAS BEEN CALLED THE "CURER OF ALL AILMENTS," THE "panacea for all diseases," and the "blessed divine," among other things. It is the neem tree. There are approximately 14 million of these trees in India alone, and more grow in the other countries of the subcontinent and in parts of West Africa. The neem, which can grow up to 50 feet tall, has been revered for its versatile traits for more than 5,000 years. The neem has been called on to treat leprosy, ulcers, and skin disorders. It has been used to make pesticides and spermicides. The tree's oil can serve as a fuel for lamps. Extracts from the neem tree can be employed as a potent insecticide that is effective against nearly 200 kinds of insects. Millions of Indians have used the tree's twigs as antiseptic toothbrushes. Some people chew neem leaves when they get up in the morning, in the hope that after 24 days of doing so, their bodies will be protected from diseases such as hypertension and diabetes. To countless South Asians, urban as well as rural, the neem tree is nature's drugstore, a virtual village pharmacy.

With neem products so useful, it is logical to think that people have made money from these products' extraction and sale. Indeed, people have. Many enterprising individuals use traditional methods to smash neem seeds, scoop the emulsion (pulp) from the top, and sell it to local farmers for use as a pesticide. Making money from the neem tree was never a problem for village entrepreneurs who hoped to earn a few rupees, either as a sideline or as a full-time occupation.

Some Indian companies have produced large quantities of neem-based pesticides, cosmetics, and medicines for wide distribution. No Indian firms have ever attempted to take ownership of their neem-extraction and development processes, however. This is because Indian law does not allow for the patenting of agricultural and medical products. The Indian government claims that because the neem tree is a product of nature, there is nothing there to be patented. A patent, the government says, requires innovation and discovery. Indians have been using homegrown methods to extract neem products for years. There's nothing new or innovative in that, the government maintains.

One country's folk medicine is another country's recent find, however. In 1995, a United States–based multinational company, W.R. Grace & Company, obtained a patent from the United States Patent and Trademark Office (USPTO) for fungicidal properties of seeds extracted from the neem tree. The company claimed that the processes it had perfected represented a "discovery" because it entailed "manipulation yielding greater and better results."[77] Grace was saying that it had gone one giant step further, building on Indian techniques to create truly novel advances. The multinational asserted that it was being new and innovative and was adding value to the extraction process. Grace owned exclusive rights to the neem-based biopesticides used on food crops that it had "developed," the company now declared.

The claims did not stop there, however. Because it was a multinational corporation, Grace said, it had the right to sue Indian companies for making the neem emulsion. Grace demanded that such companies stop producing neem-based pesticides. This United States–based multinational insisted that it had the sole, exclusive right to sell the neem extract, even in India, the home of the neem tree.

Accusations of biopiracy soon filled the air. Interestingly, the accusations came from Grace as well as from the Indian government. Once again, the WTO stood ready to enter the picture.

TRIPS

Intellectual property rights (IPRs) have been recognized for centuries. Such rights represent an attempt to foster creativity and innovation. If a company knows that it has exclusive rights to what it has created, the argument goes, society as a whole will benefit. It will benefit because the profit motive, enhanced by secure property rights, will bring on new products and services. This will be true whether the creation involves books, paintings, and films (protected by copyright); inventions and technological innovations (protected by patents); or marketing tools (logos and trademarks, also protected).

By the middle of the 1990s, if not sooner, holders of copyrights, patents, trademarks, and the like—most of whom were based in developed countries—began to feel that greater international protection was necessary to secure what they owned. The emerging world economic and trade scene, these rights holders were convinced, offered great opportunities to expand their product penetration. At the same time, however, this emerging scene signaled that the same products might be in danger of being copied or stolen.

Above, a child dances next to pirated versions of Teletubbies bags on sale at an outdoor stall in Beijing, China. China was put on a list of 14 countries that will receive special scrutiny due to rampant violations of intellectual property rights.

With the formation of the WTO, Western corporations, backed by their governments, saw an opportunity to expand the GATT's traditional focus on trade in goods to include more inclusive agreements on intellectual property rights. Thus was born a fundamental WTO agreement on what are known as trade-related aspects of intellectual property rights, or TRIPs.

The WTO's Agreement on Trade-Related Aspects of Intellectual Property Rights is designed to enforce global property rights. The agreement fixes common international rules. According to the WTO Web site, the TRIPs Agreement "establishes minimum levels of protection that each government has to give to the intellectual property of fellow WTO Members."[78]

Under this agreement, which all 152 WTO members must adhere to, each country is obligated to implement the agreement through its own domestic legislation. The United States, for example, is required to extend its patent protection from 17 to 20 years, the new international standard established under the TRIPs Agreement.

Nowhere does the extension of corporate monopoly on innovations get more controversial than in the realm of pharmaceuticals. Here is just one example: According to critics, the TRIPs Agreement impedes developing countries in their efforts to make or obtain cheap, generic drugs to fight AIDS (acquired immunodeficiency syndrome). Companies that hold patents on such drugs are naturally reluctant to allow for the dissemination of low-cost substitutes. It is true that, under the terms of the TRIPs Agreement, governments are allowed to reduce short-term costs through various exceptions that are designed to tackle public health problems. According to the TRIPs Agreement's detractors, however, "Wealthy countries—particularly the United States—and transnational pharmaceutical firms have exerted heavy pressure on developing countries against such policies."[79]

In gaining a patent for its claimed innovative neem tree extracting processes, W.R. Grace & Company was certain that the World Intellectual Property Organization (WIPO), the main global body dealing with international patents at the time the patent was sought, would provide the company with the protection it needed to press its case, should that be required. When the TRIPs Agreement was implemented, on January 1, 1995, Grace found a new, even more powerful ally in its corner. What Grace did not count on, however, was the coming together of more than 200 nongovernmental organizations (NGOs) from 35 countries to challenge the multinational corporation's claim. Grace was quick, of course, to remind India of its obligation under the TRIPs Agreement. Piracy—bio- and otherwise—is, it would seem, in the eye of the beholder.

"BABIES ARE OUR BUSINESS"

Breast-feeding or formula? The debate has gone on for decades. In developed countries, even people who champion the natural approach would be hard-pressed to find evidence that formula-fed infants are subject to serious health risks just because their mothers choose not to breast-feed. Whether a formula is bought already mixed in liquid or as a powder to which water is to be added, there is little concern in Western countries that the water used is less than pure. This is not so in many developing countries, however. There, the health hazards associated with the use of formula originate in a lack of clean water. When powdered formula is mixed with dirty water (water swarming with invasive microorganisms that no one wants to think about), babies are in jeopardy.

Indeed, according to the United Nations Children's Fund (UNICEF), 1.5 million infants die each year; in the majority of cases, these babies die from fatal infant diarrhea because artificial breast-milk is mixed with unclean water. So serious had the problem become that in 1981, a World Health Organization (WHO)/UNICEF International Code of Marketing of Breast-milk Substitutes was signed by a host of nations.[80]

In 1987, Guatemala passed a law designed to implement important provisions of the WHO/UNICEF code. The goal of the law was to encourage mothers to breast-feed. The law included prohibitions on the use of certain words and phrases, such as "equivalent to breast-milk" or "humanized breast-milk," in advertisements for infant formula. Furthermore, Guatemala, with a fairly large illiterate population, wanted pictures of chubby, healthy babies, presumably happy after having consumed breast-milk substitutes, removed from formula packages.[81]

Gerber, a U.S.-incorporated baby-products company that placed its pudgy "Gerber baby" logo on nearly everything it sold, was not happy. Gerber resisted attempts by the Guatemalan government to get the company to remove the image and add the words "Breast-milk is the best for baby." The company threatened a challenge and promised to take its case to the soon-to-become TRIPs Agreement under the WTO.[82]

According to Gerber, its "Gerber baby" was an integral part of its trademark, just as the phrase "Babies are our business" was its copyrighted slogan. The TRIPs Agreement, Gerber felt, provided the company with trademark protection, and thus the Guatemalan government could not require removal of the "Gerber baby" image from the company's packaging.

In the end, not having the million-dollar resources necessary to fight the case with the WTO, Guatemala backed down. It was, critics declared, another example of a WTO threat doing the trick, forcing an undeveloped country to withdraw its claims. Many observers, including the International Baby Food Action Network (a group that monitors compliance with the International Code of Marketing of Breast-milk Substitutes) felt that Guatemala could have won against Gerber if the country had had the funds to pursue the case.

COMPULSORY LICENSING

AIDS has been called the Black Death of our time. In one part of the world in particular, sub-Saharan Africa, the AIDS death toll is devastating. There, more than 7,000 people succumb each day to the disease. As of July 2002, 80 percent of the 28.5 million people who had died of AIDS had done so in sub-Saharan Africa, where some of the world's least developed countries, such as Zimbabwe, Zambia, Uganda, and the Democratic Republic of the Congo, are located.[83]

Drugs to prolong the lives of AIDS sufferers do exist. Such drugs—patented, for the most part, by Western-based multinational drug companies—are notoriously expensive, however. A typical AIDS drug cocktail costs more than $12,000 per year per patient. Almost no African can afford that kind of money. Clearly, in sub-Saharan Africa, licensed AIDS drugs are beyond the reach of the vast majority of those who need them the most.[84]

As was noted earlier, the World Trade Organization's TRIPs Agreement, which expands companies' property rights and thus patent protection, does offer exceptions. Under certain circumstances (such as public-health emergencies), the TRIPs Agreement permits countries to obtain drugs at vastly reduced prices. Known as compulsory licensing, this procedure allows a government to have someone else produce a patented product or process without the consent of the patent owner. To do so can mean a cost reduction, for some drugs, of 90 percent or more. The patent holder is to be compensated financially in the form of a reasonable royalty.[85]

In 1997, in response to its ever-worsening AIDS epidemic, the South African government passed the South African Medicines Act. Among other features, this law allowed the government to require compulsory licensing. The U.S pharmaceutical industry, along with pharmaceutical companies in South Africa, objected to the new law. The companies claimed that it violated aspects of the TRIPs Agreement. With a few exceptions, in which some pharmaceutical companies voluntarily gave away their rights in an attempt to fight the spread of AIDS, most of the companies insisted on their right to patent protection. They insisted, even if to do so might result in the deaths of millions of AIDS sufferers.

Drug company opposition to the South African law galvanized an impressive coalition of developing countries and NGOs into action. According to international trade expert Amrita Narlikar:

> The coalition drew a direct link between corporate greed and countless preventable HIV/AIDS-related deaths. It further pointed out that the U.S. was trying to prevent countries from using the emergency exception that TRIPs provided to save lives. Led by the African Group, developing countries and NGOs sought a ministerial declaration that clarified TRIPs

Members of the African National Congress protest outside the Pretoria High Court in Pretoria, South Africa, in 2001. Thirty-nine makers of AIDS medications brought a suit against the South African government in hopes of amending a 1997 law that favored generic drugs. One in five adults in South Africa are thought to be HIV-positive, and few people have access to expensive drugs. The companies were forced to withdraw their petition.

provisions on public health and guaranteed the right of governments to put public health and welfare before patents protection.[86]

Just such a declaration came at the WTO's ministerial meeting in Doha, Qatar, in 2001. "The TRIPs Agreement does not and should not prevent Members from taking measures to protect public health," it said. ". . . In this connection, we reaffirm the right of WTO Members to use, to the full, the provisions in the TRIPs Agreement, which provide flexibility for this purpose."[87] Amrita Narlikar went on to observe, "The Declaration will make it politically very difficult to bring a dispute against a country that uses compulsory licensing or parallel imports of patented medicines in response to public health emergencies."[88]

WHO BENEFITS?

The name for which TRIPs is the acronym was and is a misnomer. There is nothing in the TRIPs Agreement that actually is related to trade: The agreement is all about the protection of intellectual property rights. Trade agreements, especially WTO trade agreements, are supposed to liberalize the movement of goods and services across borders. Some critics argue that by concerning itself with stronger intellectual property rights, the TRIPs Agreement actually does the opposite: It restricts the movement of knowledge between countries. That said, the negotiators who set up the TRIPs Agreement demanded the insertion of the words *trade-related* ahead of the term *intellectual property*. Thus was born the phrase "Trade-Related Aspects of Intellectual Property Rights." To those who forced through TRIPs, there is, essentially, no aspect of intellectual property that is not trade related.

It is no secret that the TRIPs Agreement was the creation of the United States and other advanced industrial nations. It was they who sought monopoly status for their home-based companies by demanding copyright, trademark, and patent protection. By doing so, the industrialized nations ensured higher prices for their companies' products and services. Such monopoly power, it is said, generates higher profits. These profits, in turn, are supposed to provide the capital necessary to fund research and development.

There is no denying the need for and the importance of innovation. Many new products and practices, particularly in the medical field, have transformed the lives of billions of people. Furthermore, well-designed intellectual property rights clearly aid the innovative process. As economist Joseph Stiglitz

THE WILDLIFE TRADE

The international trade in wild things—plants and animals—is big business. The trade was worth around $300 billion in 2005, according to TRAFFIC (the Wildlife Trade Monitoring Network) and the World Wildlife Fund (WWF). If done correctly and managed properly, the legal trade in wildlife can be a boon for the poor in developing countries, providing them with subsistence and livelihood. According to Dr. Susan Lieberman, Director of the WWF's International Species Program, "Trade in wildlife products can have a significant economic impact on people's livelihoods, childhood education, and the role of women in developing countries, provided it is legal, well-managed, and sustainable."

In one case study, it was shown that Uganda's lake fisheries produce fish worth over $200 million per year and employ 135,000 fishers and 700,000 small-scale operators in processing, trade, and associated industries. Fully 2.2 percent of Uganda's export earnings, $87.5 million worth, are derived from the country's Lake Victoria fisheries.

In another case, it was found that trade in wild meat contributes up to 34 percent of household income in eastern and southern Africa. Such meat provides both an affordable source of animal protein and a livelihood for men (as hunters) and women (as traders).

Trade in Latin America in wild peccary (pig), caiman (a small, alligatorlike crocodilian), and the wool of the vicuña (a relative of the llama) can be quite productive, too. According to trade experts, "The caiman skin trade generates a low income for ranchers compared to cattle, but it can be significant for the poor and landless with few other income-generating opportunities."

(continues)

(continued)

In the Philippines, seahorse fishers and traders report that their catch contributes about 30 percent or 40 percent of their annual income. In some cases, it can reach 80 percent.

Estimates as to how many people depend on some sort of trade in wildlife for at least part of their income vary considerably. When the definition of what is traded—including such wild-derived products as medicines, food, clothing, ornamental plants, pets, and more —is a liberal one, the estimates range from 200 million people worldwide to a billion people in Asia and the Pacific alone. If habitats for these wild things are degraded significantly, the living standards of the world's poor could plummet, too.

Establishing property rights to or ownership of wildlife is key to that wildlife's sustainability. According to *The Economist*, "Allowing for the secure ownership of wildlife resources by a clearly defined group of poor people is essential for sustainable harvesting. If no public authority is able to offer secure tenure of land or resource rights to a reasonable number of people, there is little incentive to invest in long-term sustainability."

"Manage wildlife trade for better development outcomes," *WWF*. May 24, 2008. Available online at *http://www.panda.org/news_facts/newsroom/index.cfm?uNewsID=134781*.

"Just let them get on with it," *The Economist*. May 31, 2008, 64.

observes, "Drug companies claim that without strong intellectual property protection, they would have no incentive to do research. And without research, the drugs that companies in the developing world would like to imitate would not exist."[89]

Nonetheless, the rights and interests of producers need to be balanced with those of users. Stiglitz continues: "There will always be a need to balance the desire of inventors to protect their discoveries, and the incentives to which such protection gives rise, and the needs of the public, which benefits from wider access to knowledge, with a resulting increase in the pace of discovery and the lower prices that come from competition."[90]

Curiously, as Stiglitz and others point out, in the establishment of the TRIPs Agreement, negotiators had no trouble linking nontrade intellectual property with trade. Yet labor standards, to use just one example, are given no such linkage. As has been noted, workers' rights are not supposed to be part of what determines the decision to import foreign-made goods. Nonetheless, patent protection under the TRIPs Agreement is to be considered part of the trade equation.

In the end, the TRIPs Agreement in particular and the WTO in general are all about realpolitik. It is the job of Western trade negotiators to get the best deals for their countries' industries, either by gaining more market access or by asserting stronger intellectual property rights. As a senior adviser to Al Gore remarked in 2000, when the then–vice-president was running for president and had been accused of attempting to undermine the South African Medicines Act, "Obviously the Vice President's got to stick up for the commercial interests of U.S. companies."[91]

Fairness, it would seem, is not part of what trade negotiations are all about. The job of everyone in the process is to get as much as he or she can while giving up as little as necessary in return. Welcome to the real world!

The Development Agenda

Seattle, Washington, was chosen to host the WTO's Third Ministerial Conference in November 1999. This choice was made, in part, because the city's police chief, Norm Stamper, assured both local and WTO officials that he could handle any protests that might arise. Stamper was wrong. According to economic historian William Bernstein,

> A large minority of protesters, well-stocked with bottles, gas masks, crowbars, masonry hammers, and tripods from which to suspend observers above the throng, wreaked mayhem. By the third day of the conference, Seattle's finest had lost control. Mobs slashed

tires, broke windows, and looted shops, and more than a thousand attackers laid siege to a precinct house for hours before its astonished defenders dispersed the assault with tear gas and rubber bullets.[92]

From 40,000 to 50,000 protestors, representing more than 700 organizations and groups, took part. They included consumer activists, labor activists, animal-rights activists, and human-rights activists, along with Indian farmers and representatives of the Philippine peasant movement. These antiglobalists came together to voice the same message: "The WTO had gone too far in setting global rules that supported corporate interests at the expense of developing countries, the poor, the environment, workers, and consumers."[93]

Key to the demonstrators' concerns was the proposal, first unveiled two years earlier, in which the WTO sought expansion of its mandate. This expansion, detractors claimed, would only enhance the power of developed countries at the expense of less developed nations. In the end, the Seattle Ministerial Conference collapsed in disarray, unable to settle anything meaningful. Lori Wallach, in Seattle as an activist for the consumer advocacy group Public Citizen, announced into her walkie-talkie, "The WTO expansion is stopped! The people have won—there will be no new WTO round!"[94]

When trade ministers next met, in 2001, they chose Doha, Qatar, as their gathering site. Qatar, they knew, could severely limit any bothersome demonstrations.

The Doha Ministerial Conference launched the Doha Round, which soon became known as the Doha Development Agenda (DDA). The round was to have the express purpose of aiding developing countries, with the hope of making globalization more inclusive for the world's poor. In response to both the Seattle debacle and the tragedy of 9/11, there were strong feelings among many WTO members that a major gesture was needed to enhance multinational cooperation.

As of 2008, however, the DDA, begun in November 2001, has yet to reach a consensus. Tariffs, nontariff measures, labor standards, the environment, competition, investment, transparency, and patents are supposed to be on this development agenda. Another focus of the DDA is supposed to be agriculture. It is this last topic that has caused the most contention and that has, in effect, stalled negotiations. The continued subsidizing of agricultural production in the EU and the United States, which adversely affects billions of people in the world's developing economies, is at the root of the problem. Without a reduction in developed-country subsidies, critics assert, many developing countries are likely to remain in an economically disadvantageous, if not precarious, position.

FARM SUBSIDIES FOR RICH AND POOR

Television personality David Letterman and banker David Rockefeller get their "fair" share. So do 25,000 California cotton farmers who divide up $3 billion to $4 billion per year in government largesse. American farmers, particularly those with large farms, get a windfall from U.S. taxpayers that amounts to approximately $60 billion per year to grow—and sometimes not to grow—crops. The subsidies are supposed to keep the family farmer (the backbone of homespun, rural America) down on the farm and in business. When all crops are considered, however, 30,000 farms (1 percent of the total) receive almost 25 percent of the money doled out, or about $1 million per farm. Eighty-seven percent goes to the top 20 percent of farmers. A true family farmer (2,440,184 of them are at the bottom of the subsidy list) gets less than $7,000 per year. U.S. farm subsidies are big business, are for big business, and are for agribusiness.[95]

Critics against the U. S. Dairy Program state that dairy policy reform is needed to allow farmers to make a living from markets, like entrepreneurs, rather than receiving a government check. The dairy farmer above argues that fees assessed on him are helping to subsidize his competitors' imported dairy products.

Other Western countries can be just as generous, if not more so, in taking care of their farmers. More than two-thirds of farm income in Norway and Switzerland comes from subsidies. In Japan, the figure is close to half. In the EU, it is a third. According to the World Bank, the average European cow receives a subsidy of $2 per day. Because more than half of the people who live in developing countries live on less than that, as Joseph Stiglitz points out, "It appears that it is better to be a cow in Europe than to be a poor person in a developing country."[96]

Farm subsidies in developed countries increase farm output and thus lower prices for food commodities on the international market. This lowering of prices hurts millions of farmers in developing countries who are trying to compete in the export arena. As Stiglitz observes, the problem doesn't stop there, however:

> As global agricultural prices are depressed by the huge American and EU subsidies, domestic agricultural prices fall too, so that even those farmers who do not export—who only sell at home—are hurt. And lower incomes for farmers translate into lower incomes for those who sell goods to the farmers: the tailors and butchers; storekeepers and barbers. Everyone in the country suffers.[97]

Subsidies, preferential tariffs, and the like can, of course, be put in place to aid small farmers in their fight to maintain market share against the big guys. Indeed, that is what the EU has sought to do in establishing a special relationship between it and many of its former colonies in Africa, the Caribbean, and the Pacific (ACP). The EU, for example, set aside a portion of its banana market for Caribbean Island producers.

These producers grow bananas on small plots of land, usually on mountainous terrain. This results in relatively high production costs. On the open market, fruit from such producers cannot compete with fruit grown by the likes of Chiquita, Del Monte, and Dole, giant corporations that grow bananas on large plantations using cheap farm labor. Hence the EU's special treatment for its former colonies, for which banana sales can account for between 63 percent and 91 percent of export earnings.[98]

In 1996, the U.S. government, with corporate urging, filed a challenge with the WTO against the EU. The United States charged the EU with providing preferential treatment in violation of WTO rules. The United States won the case, and when the EU refused to eliminate its banana support program, the United States, with the WTO's blessing, imposed $190 million per year in trade sanctions against the European Union. The EU's willingness to withstand the large imposed sanctions is, in many minds, the only thing standing between economic survival and ruin for Caribbean farmers. A development agenda can get complicated.

THE RESOURCE CURSE

If developing countries are rich in anything other than an abundance of low-wage labor, it is natural resources. Indeed, it was for such resources—minerals, timber, agricultural goods, and, later, oil—that many of these countries were colonized by the West. The greatest part of the world's natural resources (approximately 80 percent) is consumed by a relatively small percentage of users (about 20 percent) in the developed world. The WTO, on its formation in 1995, made it a top priority to grant favorable treatment for the exporting of these resources to markets in the West. Low import tariffs were granted on raw wood products, for example, while high input tariffs were imposed on manufactured goods. At first glace, this would seem to work well for developing nations, as it allows them to export products that are, for them, clearly a comparative advantage. On closer inspection, however, two difficulties emerge: the problem of "rip-and-ship" and the "resource curse."

The WTO did not encourage the freer flow of raw materials from poorer to richer countries because the WTO sought to aid the developing world. On the contrary, the idea was to gain resources for rich countries by imposing low tariffs on raw materials from developing countries while at the same time excluding (as much as possible) competing manufactured

Although many resource-rich countries have failed to transform their natural wealth into growth, Botswana has been a marked exception to the resource curse. Its abundance of diamonds has contributed significantly to its economic growth over several decades. As a result, it has experienced good governance, political stability, and strong fiscal regulation. The country has also achieved one of the highest levels of education enrollment in the region. Above, a worker looks out over the Jwaneng diamond mine, the largest producer of gem diamonds in the world.

goods from the same developing countries by imposing high tariffs. The result, in many cases, is the "rip-and-ship" use of natural resources. The tariff structure encourages extensive, nonsustaining exploitation of a developing nation's resources even as it retards the development of domestic manufacturing industries to process the same raw materials in the nations where they originate. The system rewards, for example, the exportation of raw timber but discourages the exportation of finished furniture made from such logs.

Many developing countries, particularly those at or close to the bottom of the economic pile, also suffer from another problem of resource abundance: the "paradox of plenty." As counterintuitive as it may seem, many countries seemingly rich in natural resources, whether trees, diamonds, or oil, actually are poorer for it. They are victims of what is known as the "resource curse."

The resource curse was first described in the early 1990s, although it has existed for centuries. Here is how the curse works: When a country finds itself "in the money" because it is selling and exporting its highly desired natural resource (think oil or natural gas), its currency increases in value. Because this higher-valued currency makes exports in other sectors of the country's economy more expensive, the export value of these other products is suppressed, or reduced. This happens even when these other exports may have been the best vehicles for the country's technical progress. The resource curse, in effect, crowds out export activities that are more likely to be growth oriented—those that offer the country's citizens the chance of significant employment. In the long run, the country might have been better off if, instead of raking in money from its desirable natural resource, it had been forced to develop its infrastructure, invest in health and education, and concentrate on the export of manufactured goods.

The resource curse can lead a country to political, as well as economic, degeneration. Major conflicts, armed and otherwise, often develop as different groups fight over their share of the resource pie. Furthermore, a country rich in a single natural resource—a country in the Persian Gulf that is awash with oil, for example—will have no need to tax its citizens. As desirable as that may seem at first, it means that the citizens are in no position to demand accountability from their leaders because the citizens have not been asked to "buy in" to the country's economy. Repressive, autocratic rule is often the result.

The negative effects of the resource curse are not inevitable, of course. Countries can and have overcome the curse by creating sovereign wealth funds to manage the influx of resource wealth and by investing in education and infrastructure to increase the competitiveness of their manufacturing sectors. It is not easy for a government to do this, however, because there always will be intense political pressure to spend the boom revenues, either on grandiose show projects or to alleviate poverty.

REFORMING THE WTO

There was a time when the world easily might have been divided into two groups—developed countries and undeveloped countries, with the latter often referred to, more optimistically, as "developing," or "emerging." The population of the former consisted of the world's top billion people; the population of the latter, the bottom 5 billion people.

According to economist Paul Collier, this concept is now outdated. Indeed, to Collier, the world has flipped: About 85 percent of the planet's population of 6 billion currently lives either in developed countries or in those that, while they are still developing, have been doing so at amazing speeds. It is the bottom billion (approximately 15 percent) that are in dire straits and in need of help, Collier asserts. "We must learn to turn the familiar numbers upside down," he says. "A total of five billion people who are already prosperous, or at least are on track to be so, and one billion who are stuck at the bottom."[99]

The WTO protests in Seattle were, it would seem, primarily about the bottom billion. Yet Thomas Friedman, the author of the hugely successful book *The World is Flat*, sees the Seattle protests in a less-than-positive light. Friedman cites five factors behind the disturbances. The first four of these factors he dismisses more or less out of hand. He has little use for what he terms upper-middle-class guilt, Old Left socialism, the inability

POVERTY FACTS AND STATISTICS

Despite much progress over the past three decades, the world remains a poor place. The statistics can be sobering:

- According to UNICEF, between 26,500 and 30,000 children die each day because of poverty. Furthermore, they "die quietly in some of the poorest villages on Earth, far removed from the scrutiny and the conscience of the world. Being meek and weak in life makes these dying multitudes even more invisible in death."
- Based on enrollment data, about 72 million children of primary-school age in the developing world were not in school in 2005; 57 percent of them were girls. Moreover, these are regarded as optimistic numbers.
- Nearly a billion people entered the twenty-first century unable to read a book or sign their names.
- Number of children in the world: 2.2 billion; number in poverty: I billion (every second child).
- Some 1.8 million child deaths occur each year as a result of diarrhea.
- Some 443 million school days are lost each year as a result of water-related illnesses.
- Approximately half of the world's population now lives in cites and towns. In 2005, one out of three urban dwellers, or approximately I billion people, lived in slum conditions.
- More than 80 percent of the world's population lives in countries where income differentials between rich and poor are widening.
- In developing countries, some 2.5 billion people are forced to rely on biomass—fuelwood, charcoal, and animal

(continues)

(continued)

dung—to meet their energy needs for cooking. In sub-Saharan Africa, more than 80 percent of the population depends on traditional biomass for cooking, as does more than half of the populations of India and China.

- In 2006, the world's population was approximately 6.5 billion people. That same year, world gross domestic product—the total market value of the goods and services that a country or countries produce in a specific period—was $48.2 trillion. The wealthiest countries, with a total population of approximately 1 billion people, accounted for $36.6 trillion, or 76 percent. Low-income countries, with a total population of about 2.4 billion people, accounted for just $1.6 trillion, or 3.3 percent. Middle-income countries, with a total population of about 3 billion people, made up the rest of the world's GDP at just over $10 trillion, or 20.7 percent.

Anup Shah, "Causes of Poverty: Poverty Facts and Stats." Available online at *http://www.globalissues.org/TradeRelated/Facts.asp?p=1*.

to deal with rapid change, or anti-Americanism as justifications for protest. He has more respect for a fifth force at work in Seattle: There, activists showed genuine concern with how globalization is to proceed, rather than concern about whether it is to go forward at all.

There is little doubt, however (Friedman's judgment aside) that the activists at Seattle also were protesting the genuine inequality and hypocrisy of the advanced industrial countries, those whose power and influence have allowed them to dominate the WTO. "While these countries had preached—and forced—the opening of the markets in the developing countries to their industrial products, they had continued to keep their markets closed to the products of developing countries, such as textiles and agriculture," Joseph Stiglitz notes. "While they preached that developing countries should not subsidize their industries, they continued to provide billions in subsidies to their own farmers, making it impossible for the developing countries to compete."[100]

Clearly, the WTO is in need of reform. Developing countries, particularly those that still struggle mightily, perceive a genuine disenfranchisement: They see a WTO with an institutional structure that works against them. Yet, as Amrita Narlikar, in reference to developing nations, points out with regard to a possible WTO meltdown,

> It has taken them [developing nations] a long time to learn to operate within the multilateral forum of the GATT/WTO, and they are now finally beginning to do so with some panache through the newfound strength of their coalitions. They would find themselves exposed to unprecedented bilateral pressures from the developed countries against which they would have no institutional protection. The WTO is all that they have against the use of unmitigated power, and it is in their own interests to ensure its strength and survival.[101]

FAILURE AND SUCCESS

Both are African countries, thousands of miles south of the Sahara Desert. Both are landlocked—no ships brimming with imports and exports sail into or out of their nonexistent harbors. They share a common 500-mile-long border, much of it defined by the Zambezi River. Yet Zimbabwe, to the east, and Botswana, to the west, have taken decidedly different directions toward democracy and development since they achieved independence from British rule, the former in 1980, the latter in 1966. Today, Botswana is Africa's oldest democracy. Zimbabwe, despite its democratic trappings, is anything but a free society.

It was two days before Zimbabwe's scheduled presidential runoff election on June 27, 2008. Armed youths by the thousands roamed the streets of the country's capital, Harare, proclaiming their support for autocratic president Robert Mugabe and threatening to kill supporters of rival Morgan Tsvangirai. "Don't vote for Tsvangirai or the youth will kill you," a leader representing Mugabe told terrified gatherings of opposition supporters. "We have got strong youth and we are not joking. We are serious. This is not America."[102]

Zimbabwe, a founding member of the WTO, is not only an international pariah because of its human rights abuses; it is also a country in economic free fall. Despite Zimbabwe's ascension to the WTO in 1995, when the country agreed to "lock in" trade liberalization measures advocated by the WTO, economically, the country has suffered grievously. Hyperinflation reached 100,000 percent in 2008; Zimbabwean consumers carried bags of money around to purchase simple necessities. Unemployment reached 80 percent, and the country's dollar was basically worthless. According to the World Heath Organization, Zimbabwe has the world's lowest life expectancy.[103]

What a difference a river-crossing can make. Botswana has held free elections every five years since the country's formation over four decades ago. Between 1970 and 1990, Botswana had the fortunate distinction of having the highest economic growth rate in the world—13 percent per year. Today, its growth numbers have declined to a still quite respectable 5 percent to 6 percent. Inflation hovers at around 7 percent. Botswana—whose main export product, diamonds, needs no expensive port to ship out from, but can fly forth on any aircraft—has, according to *Time* magazine correspondent Alex Perry, beaten the resource curse. "Botswana," he declares, "the world's biggest producer of diamonds, has proved an exception to this rule [the resource curse], raising its 1.9 million people out of poverty within the span of a generation."[104] According to the International Monetary Fund, Botswana has graduated to middle-income status.

The country has problems, of course, not the least of which is the devastation that AIDS has inflicted on its population. With 37.5 percent of its residents infected, Botswana's very future is in jeopardy. Yet, with the help of international donors, Botswana launched an ambitious national campaign that provided free antiviral drugs to anyone who needed them. By March 2004, Botswana's infection rate had dropped significantly.[105]

Botswana, like Zimbabwe, was a founding member of the WTO. It has been a dutiful WTO player in many respects. According to the WTO's Web site, "Botswana's new foreign trade policy is aimed at achieving free and dependable access for its exports and lowering the cost of importing goods by reducing tariffs and trade barriers."[106] According to the WTO mandate, this is just what every good trading member should do.

Botswana has followed the WTO script only to a point, however. When the deals appeared to be advantageous, the country has entered into agreements that have given it special treatment for its diamond and beef exports. In a successful attempt to mitigate the resource curse, Botswana prudently put aside reserve funds from the sale of diamonds and beef for the rainy day that always comes. The country also negotiated with one of the world's most powerful multinationals, the diamond cartel De Beers, to get its share of revenues boosted from 15 percent to 50 percent. Botswana—a developing country shrewdly negotiating its options, enhancing the welfare of its people, and eagerly trading and bartering on the world stage—is the kind of developing country that the WTO can expect to see a lot more of in the years to come.

CHRONOLOGY

1947   **October** Twenty-three countries sign the General Agreement on Tariffs and Trade (GATT) in Geneva, Switzerland, to try and give an early boost to post–World War II trade liberalization.

1948   **January 1** GATT is formally established.

1948–1979   Seven rounds of GATT negotiations take place, with an emphasis on tariff reductions and antidumping measures.

1986–1994   A seven-and-a-half-year round of negotiations culminates in the decision to establish the World Trade Organization (WTO).

1995   **January 1** The WTO is officially created in Geneva, Switzerland. Intellectual property rights are high on the new organization's agenda.

1996   **December** At the first WTO ministerial meeting, held in Singapore, developing countries reject the establishment of any linkage between labor standards and trade rules.

1998   **May** At the second WTO ministerial meeting, held in Geneva, Switzerland, members pledge, in the wake of the East Asian financial crisis, to reject protectionism and "keep all markets open."

1999   **November** The third WTO ministerial meeting, held in Seattle, Washington, results in the "Battle of Seattle," in which thousands of protestors, spearheaded by environmentalists and some U.S. labor unions, essentially shut down the meeting.

2001   **November** The fourth WTO ministerial meeting, held in Doha, Qatar, just two months after the September 11 terrorist attacks, seeks to demonstrate North-South solidarity in the face of terrorism.

The Doha Development Agenda (DDA) or Doha Round is launched. The GATT/WTO ninth trade round is intended to help developing countries but, to date, has failed to achieve success.

December The People's Republic of China joins the WTO after 15 years of negotiations (the longest in GATT/WTO history).

2002 **August** The WTO rules that the EU can impose up to $4 billion in sanctions on U.S. goods after winning a dispute over U.S. government tax breaks for American exporters. These are the highest damages ever awarded by the WTO.

2003 **September** The WTO announces a deal aimed at giving developing countries access to cheap medicines, particularly AIDS medications.

September The fifth WTO ministerial meeting, held in Cancun, Mexico, collapses after arguments highlight the sharp differences between rich and poor nations in terms of agriculture and global investment issues.

2005 **December** The sixth WTO ministerial meeting, held in Hong Kong, fails to reach a breakthrough in trade negotiations.

2006 **October** The United States and Russia reach an agreement in principle on a bilateral market access deal in the context of Russia's efforts to join the WTO.

2008 **May** Ukraine becomes the 152nd member of the WTO.

NOTES

Introduction

1. Clarence Fernandez, "Simple Strategies Could Save Malaysia Sea Turtles," *Reuters*, July 20, 2007. Available online at http://www.reuters.com/article/environmentNews/id USKLR11194120070720.

2. "WTO and Sea Turtles Clash Again and Again," *Animal Welfare Institute Quarterly*, Summer 2001, vol. 50, no. 3, 1–2.

3. "India etc. versus US: 'shrimp-turtle,'" *World Trade Organization*. Available online at http://www.wto.org/english/tratop_e/envir_e/edis08_e.htm.

4. Ibid., 2.

5. Dieter Braeuninger, "Has Globalization Deepened Inequality?" *YaleGlobal*, February 6, 2008. Available online at http://yaleglobal.yale.edu/display.article?id=10309.

Chapter 1

6. William J. Bernstein, *A Splendid Exchange: How Trade Shaped the World*. New York: Atlantic Monthly Press, 2008, 69.

7. Ibid., 98.

8. Frank Viviano, "China's Great Armada," *National Geographic*, July 2005, 52.

9. Daniel J. Boorstin, *The Discoverers: A History of Man's Search to Know His World and Himself*. New York: Random House, 1983, 177.

10. Adam Smith, *An Inquiry into the Nature and Causes of the Wealth of Nations*. Chicago: University of Chicago Press, 1976, I: 17.

11. "Smoot-Hawley Tariff," *U.S. Department of State*. Available online at http://future.state.gov/when/timeline/1921_time line/smoot_tariff.html

12.   "Who Was Cordell Hull?" *Cordell Hull Institute*. Available online at http://www.cordellhullinstitute.org/role/who.html.

13.   William J. Bernstein, *A Splendid Exchange*, 352–353.

Chapter 2

14.   Eric Schlosser, *Fast Food Nation: The Dark Side of the All-American Meal*. New York: Houghton Mifflin Company, 2001, 4.

15.   "Big Bite," *The Economist*, April 24, 2008, 107.

16.   "The Global 2000," *Forbes*, April 21, 2008, 196.

17.   Dar Haddix, "Faces of Globalization—Pollo Campero," *Global Envision*, August 16, 2004, 1–2.

18.   "Selling Rhythm to the World," *The Economist*, March 27, 2008, 52.

19.   "Work In, Cash Out," *Time*, May 19, 2008, 14–15.

20.   Marla Dickerson and Tiffany Hsu, "Economy crimps flow of funds over border," *Los Angeles Times*, March 12, 2008, C1.

21.   Manfred B. Steger, *Globalization: A Very Short Introduction*. New York: Oxford University Press, 2003, 13.

22.   Dieter Braeuninger, "Has Globalization Deepened Inequality?" *YaleGlobal*, February 6, 2008. Available online at http://yaleglobal.yale.edu/display.article?id=10309.

23.   "Globalization with Few Discontents?" *YaleGlobal*, June 3, 2003. Available online at http://yaleglobal.yale.edu/display.article?id=1764.

24.   Thomas L. Friedman, *The World is Flat: A Brief History of the Twenty-First Century*. New York: Farrar, Straus and Giroux, 2005, 114.

25.   Joseph E. Stiglitz, *Globalization and Its Discontents*. New York: W.W. Norton & Company, 2003, 21.

26. "Is Globalisation Killing India's Cotton Farmers?" *The Economist*, January 18, 2007, 63.

27. Michel Chossudovsky, "Global Falsehoods." Available online at http://www.canadianliberty.bc.ca/relatedinfo/globalpoverty.html.

28. Anup Shah, "Poverty Facts and Stats." Available online at http://www.globalissues.org/TradeRelated/Facts.asp?p=1.

29. Roger Cohen, "The Global Rose as a Social Tool," *New York Times*, March 13, 2008, 1.

30. Joseph E. Stiglitz, *Making Globalization Work*. New York: W.W. Norton & Company, 2006, 9.

Chapter 3

31. Amrita Narlikar, *The World Trade Organization: A Very Short Introduction*. New York: Oxford University Press, 2005, 12.

32. Ibid., 33.

33. Ibid., 57–58.

34. Joseph E. Stiglitz, *Globalization and its Discontents*, 19.

35. Peter Montagne, "Making Sense out of the WTO," *Rachel's Environment & Health Weekly* #679, 3. Available online at http://www.rachel.org/en/node/4975.

Chapter 4

36. "Threats to the Bottlenose Dolphin and Other Marine Mammals," *The Dolphin Institute*, 2002. Available online at http://www.dolphin-institute.org/resource_guide/conservation.htm.

37. "Tuna-Dolphin Issue," *Encyclopedia of Marine Mammals*. San Diego: Academic Press, 2002, 1269–1273.

38. Lori Wallach and Patrick Woodall, *Whose Trade Organization?* New York: The New Press, 2004, 30.

39. Ibid., 29.

40. Lori Wallach and Patrick Woodall, *Whose Trade Organization?*, 39.

41. James Stone, "Resolving the Animal Welfare and Legal Issues of the EU Fur Import Prohibition; View of Canada," January 17, 1997, 2. Available online at http://www.high north.no/Library/Trade/GATT_WTO/re-th-an.htm

42. Ibid., 2.

43. Ibid., 3.

44. Lori Wallach and Patrick Woodall, *Whose Trade Organization?*, 37.

45. Ibid., 63.

46. Gary P. Sampson, *Trade, Environment, and the WTO: The Post-Seattle Agenda.* Washington, D.C.: Johns Hopkins University Press, 2000, 52.

47. Ibid., 58.

Chapter 5

48. David Barboza, "In Chinese Factories, Lost Fingers and Low Pay," *New York Times*, January 5, 2008. Business, 3.

49. Ibid., 2.

50. Nicholas D. Kristof and Sheryl Wudunn, "Two Cheers for Sweatshops," *New York Times* Magazine, September 24, 2000, 1.

51. Ibid., 2.

52. Brendan January, *Globalize It!* Brookfield: Twenty-First Century Books, 2003, 39.

53. S.L. Bachman, "Nike v. Sweatshop Critic: Back to California," *YaleGlobal*, June 27, 2003, 2.

54. David L. Parker, "Before Their Time: Child Labor Around the World," *American Educator*, Spring 2008, 38.

55. Ibid., 39–41.

56. David Barboza, "China Says Abusive Child Labor Ring Is Exposed," *New York Times*, May 1, 2008, 1, 5.

57. Joseph E. Stiglitz, *Making Globalization Work*, 187–188.

58. Ibid., 188.

59. William J. Holstein, "Emerging Markets, Emerging Giants," *New York Times*, April 22, 2007, 2–3.

60. Justin Fox, "A Port That Exports," *Time*, June 9, 2008, 37.

61. "Economic Focus," *The Economist*, April 19, 2008, 92.

62. Lori Wallach and Patrick Woodall, *Whose Trade Organization?*, 227.

63. Ibid., 228.

Chapter 6

64. Terry Devitt, "The Beef War," *The Why? Files*, p. 2. Available online at http://whyfiles.org/088beef/.

65. Ibid., 2

66. Lori Wallach and Patrick Woodall, *Whose Trade Organization?*, 71.

67. "Sanitary and Phytosanitary Measures," *World Trade Organization*. Available online at http://www.wto.org/english/tratop_e/sps_e/spsund_e.htm.

68. Terry Devitt, "The Beef War," *The Why? Files*, p.3. Available online at http://whyfiles.org/088beef/.

69. "What's wrong with the WTO?" Available online at http://www.speakeasy.org/~peterc/wtow/.

70. Lori Wallach and Michelle Sforza, *The WTO: Five Years of Reasons to Resist Corporate Globalization*. New York: Seven Stories Press, 1999, 44.

71. Lori Wallach and Patrick Woodall, *Whose Trade Organization?*, 90.

72. Ibid., 91.

73. Bhagirath Lal Das, *The World Trade Organisation: A Guide to the Framework for International Trade*. London: Zed Books Ltd., 1999, 120.

74. Lori Wallach and Patrick Woodall, *Whose Trade Organization?*, 63.

75. "Understanding the WTO: The Agreements, Standards and Safety." Available online at http://www.wto.org/english/thewto_e/whatis_e/tif_e/agrm4_e.htm.

76. Ibid.

Chapter 7

77. Sara Hasan, "The Neem Tree, Environment, Culture and Intellectual Property," *TED Case Studies* No. 665, 4, 2002. Available online at http://www.american.edu/TED/neemtree.htm.

78. Bhagirath Lal Das, *The World Trade Organisation*, 357.

79. "You Must Treat Life Forms and Life-Saving Drugs as Commodities," *What's Wrong with the WTO?* Available online at http://www.speakeasy.org/~peterc/wtow/wto-trip.htm.

80. Lori Wallach and Patrick Woodall, *Whose Trade Organization?*, 92.

81. Ibid.

82. Ibid., 93.

83. Lori Wallach and Patrick Woodall, *Whose Trade Organization?*, 94.

84. Ibid.

85. "WTO Summit: Don't Undercut AIDS Drug Access," *Human Rights Watch*. 2006, 2. Available online at http://www.hrw.org/en/news/2001/11/06/wto-summit-dont-undercut-aids-drug-access.

86. Amrita Narlikar, *The World Trade Organization*, 107.

87. Ibid., 105.

88. Ibid.

89. Joseph E. Stiglitz. *Making Globalization Work*, 106.

90. Ibid.

91. Lori Wallach and Patrick Woodall, *Whose Trade Organization?*, 96.

Chapter 8

92. William J. Bernstein, *A Splendid Exchange*, 366.

93. Manfred B. Steger, *Globalization: A Very Short Introduction*. New York: Oxford University Press, 123.

94. Lori Wallach and Patrick Woodall, *Whose Trade Organization?*, 7.

95. Joseph E. Stiglitz, *Making Globalization Work*, 86.

96. Ibid., 85.

97. Ibid., 86.

98. Lori Wallach and Michelle Sforza, *The WTO*, 58.

99. Paul Collier. *The Bottom Billion*. New York: Oxford University Press, 2007, 3.

100. Joseph E. Stiglitz, *Globalization and Its Discontents*, 244.

101. Amrita Narlikar, *The World Trade Organization*, 137–138.

102. "Ballot Box Death Threats," *Los Angeles Times*, June 25, 2008, 1.

103. Christian Nordquist, "Zimbabwe Life Expectancy Lowest in the World." Available online at http://www.medical newstoday.com/articles/41339.php.

104. Alex Perry, "Gem of an Idea," *Time*, May 12, 2008, 10.

105. "Botswana." Available online at http://www.infoplease. com/ipa/A0107353.html.

106. Kennedy K. Mbekeani, "Inter-Agency Policy Coordination in Botswana," *World Trade Organization*. Available at http://www.wto.org/english/res_e/booksp_ e/casestudies_e/case6_e.htm.

BIBLIOGRAPHY

Bachman, S.L. "Nike v. Sweatshop Critic: Back to California." *YaleGlobal*, June 27, 2003, 2.

"Ballot Box Death Threats." *Los Angeles Times*, June 25, 2008, 1.

Barboza, David. "China Says Abusive Child Labor Ring Is Exposed." *New York Times*, May 1, 2008, 1, 5.

————. "In Chinese Factories, Lost Fingers and Low Pay." *New York Times*, Business, January 5, 2008, 3.

Barnet, Richard J., and John Cavanagh. *Global Dreams: Imperial Corporations and the New World Order*. New York: Simon & Schuster, 1994.

Bernstein, William J. *A Splendid Exchange: How Trade Shaped the World*. New York: Atlantic Monthly Press, 2008.

"Big Bite." *The Economist*, April 24, 2008, 107.

Boorstin, Daniel J. *The Discoverers: A History of Man's Search to Know His World and Himself*. New York: Random House, 1983.

"Botswana." Available online at http://www.infoplease.com/ipa/A0107353.html.

Braeuninger, Dieter. "Has Globalization Deepened Inequality?" *YaleGlobal*, February 6, 2008. Available online at http://yaleglobal.yale.edu/display.article?id=10309.

Chossudovsky, Michel. "Global Falsehoods." Available online at http://www.canadianliberty.bc.ca/relatedinfo/globalpoverty.html.

Cohen, Roger. "The Global Rose as a Social Tool." *New York Times*, March 13, 2008, 1.

Collier, Paul. *The Bottom Billion: Why the Poorest Countries Are Failing and What Can Be Done About it*. New York: Oxford University Press, 2007.

Dasgupta, Partha. *Economics: A Very Short Introduction*. New York: Oxford University Press, 2007.

Devitt, Terry. "The Beef War." *The Why? Files*. Available online at http://whyfiles.org/088beef/.

Dickerson, Marla and Tiffany Hsu. "Economy crimps flow of funds over border." *Los Angeles Times*, March 12, 2008, C1.

"Economic Focus." *The Economist*, April 19, 2008, 92.

Fernandez, Clarence. "Simple Strategies Could Save Malaysia Sea Turtles." *Reuters*, July 20, 2007. Available online at http://www.reuters.com/article/environmentNews/idUSKLR111941 20070720.

Flynn, Sean Masaki. *Economics for Dummies*. Hoboken, NJ: Wiley Publishing, Inc., 2005.

Fox, Justin. "A Port That Exports." *Time*, June 9, 2008, 37.

Friedman, Thomas L. *The World is Flat: A Brief History of the Twenty-First Century*. New York: Farrar, Straus and Giroux, 2005.

Fulcher, James. *Capitalism: A Very Short Introduction*. New York: Oxford University Press, 2004.

"Globalization with Few Discontents?" *YaleGlobal*, June 3, 2003. Available online at http://yaleglobal.yale.edu/display.article?id=1764.

Haddix, Dar. "Faces of Globalization—Pollo Campero." *Global Envision*, August 16, 2004, 1–2.

Hasan, Sara. "The Neem Tree, Environment, Culture and Intellectual Property." *TED Case Studies* No. 665, 4, 2002. Available online at http://www.american.edu/TED/neemtree.htm.

Holstein, William J. "Emerging Markets, Emerging Giants." *New York Times*, April 22, 2007, 2–3.

"India etc. versus US: 'shrimp-turtle.'" *World Trade Organization*. Available online at http://www.wto.org/english/tratop_e/envir_e/edis08_e.htm.

"Is Globalisation Killing India's Cotton Farmers?" *The Econo-mist*, January 18, 2007, 63.

January, Brendan. *Globalize It! The Stories of the IMF, the World Bank, the WTO—and Those Who Protest.* Brookfield, Conn.: Twenty-First Century Books, 2003.

Kristof, Nicholas D., and Sheryl Wudunn. "Two Cheers for Sweatshops." *New York Times* Magazine, September 24, 2000, 1.

Lal Das, Bhagirath. *The World Trade Organisation: A Guide to the Framework for International Trade.* London: Zed Books Ltd., 1999.

"Making Sense out of the WTO." *Rachel's Environment & Health Weekly* #679.3. Available online at http://www.rachel.org/en/node/4975.

Mander, Jerry and Edward Goldsmith, eds. *The Case Against the Global Economy and for a Turn Toward the Local.* San Francisco: Sierra Club Books, 1996.

Mbekeani, Kennedy K. "Inter-Agency Policy Co-ordination in Botswana." *World Trade Organization.* Available online at http://www.wto.org/english/res_e/booksp_e/casestudies_e/case6_e.htm.

Narlikar, Amrita. *The World Trade Organization: A Very Short Introduction.* New York: Oxford University Press, 2005.

Nordquist, Christian. "Zimbabwe Life Expectancy Lowest in the World." Available online at http://www.medicalnewstoday.com/articles/41339.php.

Olson, Elizabeth. "A Modern French Aristocrat in Trade's Fractious Arena." *New York Times*, February 10, 2000. Available online at http://query.nytimes.com/gst/fullpage.html?res=9B07E5DE133EF933A25751C0A9669C8B63.

Parker, David L. "Before Their Time: Child Labor Around the World." *American Educator*, Spring 2008, 38.

Perry, Alex. "Gem of an Idea." *Time*, May 12, 2008, 10.

Sampson, Gary P. *Trade, Environment, and The WTO: The Post-Seattle Agenda*. Washington, D.C.: Johns Hopkins University Press, 2000.

"Sanitary and Phytosanitary Measures." *World Trade Organization*. Available online at http://www.wto.org/english/tratop_e/sps_e/spsund_e.htm.

Schlosser, Eric. *Fast Food Nation: The Dark Side of the All-American Meal*. New York: Houghton Mifflin Company, 2001.

"Selling Rhythm to the World." *The Economist*, March 27, 2008, 52.

Shah, Anup. "Poverty Facts and Stats." Available online at http://www.globalissues.org/TradeRelated/Facts.asp?p=1.

Smith, Adam. *An Inquiry into the Nature and Causes of the Wealth of Nations*. Chicago, Ill.: University of Chicago Press, 1976.

"Smoot-Hawley Tariff." *U.S. Department of State*. Available online at http://future.state.gov/when/timeline/1921_timeline/smoot_tariff.html

Steger, Manfred B. *Globalization: A Very Short Introduction*. New York: Oxford University Press, 2003.

Stiglitz, Joseph E. *Globalization and Its Discontents*. New York: W.W. Norton & Company, 2003.

———. *Making Globalization Work*. New York: W.W. Norton & Company, 2006.

Stone, James. "Resolving the Animal Welfare and Legal Issues of the EU Fur Import Prohibition; View of Canada." January 17, 1997. Available online at http://www.highnorth.no/Library/Trade/GATT_WTO/re-th-an.htm.

"The Global 2000." *Forbes*, April 21, 2008, 196.

"Tuna-Dolphin Issue." *Encyclopedia of Marine Mammals*. San Diego: Academic Press, 2002.

"Threats to the Bottlenose Dolphin and Other Marine Mammals." *The Dolphin Institute*, 2002. Available online at http://www.dolphin-institute.org/resource_guide/conservation.htm.

"Understanding the WTO: The Agreements, Standards and Safety." Available online at http://www.wto.org/english/the wto_e/whatis_e/tif_e/agrm4_e.htm.

Viviano, Frank. "China's Great Armada." *National Geographic*, July 2005, 52.

Wallach, Lori and Michelle Sforza. *The WTO: Five Years of Reasons to Resist Corporate Globalization*. New York: Seven Stories Press, 1999.

Wallach, Lori and Patrick Woodall. *Whose Trade Organization?* New York: The New Press, 2004.

"What's wrong with the WTO?" Available online at http://www.speakeasy.org/~peterc/wtow/.

"Who was Cordell Hull?" *Cordell Hull Institute*. Available online at http://www.cordellhullinstitute.org/role/who.html.

Wolf, Martin. *Why Globalization Works*. New Haven, Conn.: Yale University Press, 2004.

"Work In, Cash Out." *Time*, May 19, 2008, 14–15.

"WTO and Sea Turtles Clash Again and Again." *Animal Welfare Institute Quarterly*. Summer 2001, vol. 50, no. 3, 1–2.

"WTO Summit: Don't Undercut AIDS Drug Access." *Human Rights Watch*, 2006. Available online at http://www.hrw.org/en/news/2001/11/06/wto_summit_dont_undercut_aids_drug_access.

"You Must Treat Life Forms and Life-Saving Drugs as Commodities." *What's Wrong with the WTO?* Available online at http://www.speakeasy.org/~peterc/wtow/wto-trip.htm.

Ballard, Nadejda. *Globalization and Poverty*. New York: Chelsea House, 2005.

Cooper, Adrian. *Fair Trade?* London: Franklin Watts Ltd., 2008.

David, Laurie and Cambria Gordon. *The Down-to-Earth Guide To Global Warming*. New York: Scholastic, 2007.

Enderwick, Peter. *Globalization and Labor*. New York: Chelsea House, 2005.

Flynn, Sean Masaki. *Economics for Dummies*. Hoboken, NJ: Wiley Publishing, Inc., 2005.

Gifford, Clive. *The Arms Trade*. London: Chrysalis Children's Books, 2004.

Hastings, Terry. *The Peace Corps*. New York: Chelsea House, 2005.

Hibbert, Adam. *Globalization*. New York: Raintree, 2005.

Jaffe, Eugene D. *Globalization and Development*. New York: Chelsea House, 2005.

January, Brendan. *Globalize It! The Stories of the IMF, the World Bank, the WTO—and Those Who Protest*. Brookfield, Conn.: Twenty-First Century Books, 2003.

WEB SITES

Disinformation: World Trade Organization
http://www.disinfo.com/archive/pages/dossier/id216/pg1/

Disinformation is a search service for those looking for information on current affairs, politics, new science, and "hidden information" that is seldom reported in detail by the traditional media.

50 Years Is Enough
http://www.50years.org/

50 Years is Enough: U.S. Network for Global Economic Justice is a coalition of over 200 U.S. grassroots, women's, solidarity, faith-based, policy, social- and economic-justice, youth, labor, and development organizations dedicated to the transformation of the World Bank and the International Monetary Fund (IMF).

Globalization101.org
http://www.globalization101.org/What_is_Globalization.html

Globalization 101 is an Internet resource offered by the Levin Institute that is devoted to a better understanding of what globalization is and, as a result, challenges one to think about its many controversies and trade-offs.

Global Policy Forum
http://www.globalpolicy.org/ngos/index.htm

Global Policy Form (GPF) monitors policy making at the United Nations, promotes accountability of global decisions, educates and mobilizes for global citizen participation, and advocates on vital issues of international peace and justice.

ImportGenius.com
http://www.importgenius.com/?gclid=Cli08aiFtpQCFRJxxwodlXPVTw

Import Genius provides detailed shipment data for every container that enters the United States. It claims to have the world's most powerful and accessible database of international trade intelligence.

International Forum on Globalization
http://www.ifg.org/

The International Forum on Globalization (IFG) is a North-South research and educational institution composed of leading activists, economists, scholars, and researchers providing analyses and critiques on the cultural, social, political, and environmental impacts of economic globalization.

NGO Global Network
http://www.ngo.org/ngo5.htm

NGO Global Network is a site with links to non-governmental organizations associated with the United Nations.

Oxfam International
http://www.oxfam.org

Oxfam International is a confederation of 13 like-minded organizations working together and with partners and allies around the world to bring about lasting change. They work directly with communities and seek to influence the powerful to ensure that poor people can improve their lives and livelihoods and have a say in decisions that affect them.

The US-China Business Council
http://www.uschina.org/public/wto/

The US-China Business Council, Inc. (USCBC) is a private, nonpartisan, nonprofit organization of roughly 250 American companies that do business with China.

World Trade Organization
http://www.wto.org

This is the official site for the World Trade Organization (WTO).

Worldwide NGO Directory
http://www.wango.org/resources.aspx?section=ngodir

The World Association of Non-Governmental Organizations (WANGO) is an international organization uniting

NGOs worldwide in the cause of advancing peace and global well-being. WANGO helps to provide the mechanism and support needed for NGOs to connect, partner, share, inspire, and multiply their contributions to solve humanity's basic problems.

PICTURE CREDITS

INDEX

ABOUT THE CONTRIBUTORS

Author **RONALD A. REIS** is the Technology Department Chair at Los Angeles Valley College. He has a bachelor's degree in applied technology and a master's degree in the social sciences. He is the author of 10 books for Facts On File and Chelsea House, including *The Dust Bowl*, *The Empire State Building*, *African Americans and the Civil War*, and biographies of Eugenie Clark, Jonas Salk, Lou Gehrig, Mickey Mantle, and Ted Williams. In the 1960s, he served as a Peace Corps volunteer in Malaysia.

Series editor **PEGGY KAHN** is a professor of political science at the University of Michigan-Flint, where she teaches world and European politics. She has been a social studies volunteer in the Ann Arbor, Michigan, public schools, and she helps prepare college students to become teachers. She has a Ph.D. in political science from the University of California-Berkeley and a B.A. in history and government from Oberlin College. She has lived in Europe and visited South Africa.